# Options Trading for Beginners

*The Latest Complete Guide 2019/20, All the Systems, Tips, and Strategies, Explained Step by Step in a Simple and Practical Way, Start Now and Invest in Options Trading.*

**Brian Johnson**

© Copyright 2019 by Brian Johnson - All rights reserved.

This eBook is provided with the sole purpose of providing relevant information on a specific topic for which every reasonable effort has been made to ensure that it is both accurate and reasonable. Nevertheless, by purchasing this eBook you consent to the fact that the author, as well as the publisher, are in no way experts on the topics contained herein, regardless of any claims as such that may be made within. As such, any suggestions or recommendations that are made within are done so purely for entertainment value. It is recommended that you always consult a professional prior to undertaking any of the advice or techniques discussed within.

This is a legally binding declaration that is considered both valid and fair by both the Committee of Publishers Association and the American Bar Association and should be considered as legally binding within the United States.

The reproduction, transmission, and duplication of any of the content found herein, including any specific or extended information will be done as an illegal act regardless of the end form the information ultimately takes. This includes copied versions of the work both physical, digital and audio unless express consent of the Publisher is provided beforehand. Any additional rights reserved.

Furthermore, the information that can be found within the pages described forthwith shall be considered both accurate and truthful when it comes to the recounting of facts. As such, any use, correct or incorrect, of the provided information will render the Publisher free of responsibility as to the actions taken outside of their direct purview. Regardless, there are zero scenarios where the original author or the Publisher can be deemed liable in any fashion for any damages or hardships that may result from any of the information discussed herein.

Additionally, the information in the following pages is intended only for informational purposes and should thus be thought of as universal. As befitting its nature, it is presented without assurance regarding its prolonged validity or interim quality. Trademarks that are mentioned are done without written consent and can in no way be considered an endorsement from the trademark holder.

# Table of Contents

**Chapter 1: The Basics of Options Trading** ............................ 1

**Chapter 2: The Types of Options Trading** ........................... 5

**Chapter 3: The Advantages of Trading in Options** ............ 10

    Capital Outlay and Cost Efficiency ....................................... 11

    Risk and Reward .................................................................. 12

    Flexibility and Versatility ...................................................... 13

**Chapter 4: The Components of an Option Contract** .......... 14

    Underlying Asset .................................................................. 14

    Type of Trading Option ........................................................ 15

    Strike Price ........................................................................... 16

    Premium Price ..................................................................... 17

    Expiration Date .................................................................... 18

    Settlement Option ................................................................ 18

**Chapter 5: The Fundamentals of the Pricing Options** ........ 19

    Assumptions and Consideration of Optional Pricing ............ 22

**Chapter 6: How to Start Trading in Options** ...................... 24

    Steps of Optional Trading for a Beginner ............................ 27

**Chapter 7: The Platforms and Tools for Trading Options** .. 29

    Which Are the Tools Known in the Optional Trading Is the Charts ................................................................................................ 32

**Chapter 8: Leverage** .............................................................. 34

    Types of Leverages ............................................................... 35

        *Operating Leverage* ........................................................ 36

        *Financial Leverage* ......................................................... 37

        *Combined Leverage* ....................................................... 38

*Working Capital Leverage* .................................................................. 38

## Chapter 9: Why Leverage can be Riskier ........................ 39

Limited Growth ........................................................................ 40

Losing Assets ........................................................................... 40

Inability to Get More Financing ............................................ 41

An Investor Will Not Be in a Position to Attract Equity ........ 42

Multiple as Well as Constant Losses .................................... 42

## Chapter 10: The Advantage of Trading with Leverage ....... 44

Increase in Profit ..................................................................... 45

An Increase in Capital Efficiency ........................................... 46

Is a Tool that Mitigates Against Low Volatility ..................... 47

Low Cost of Entry ................................................................... 47

## Chapter 11: The Disadvantages of Trading Leverage Options ......................................................................................... 49

Lower Liquidity ....................................................................... 49

High Spreads ........................................................................... 50

Higher Commissions ............................................................... 51

Complicated ............................................................................ 51

Time Decay .............................................................................. 52

Less Information ..................................................................... 53

Availability ............................................................................... 53

## Chapter 12: How Much Leverage It Takes to Trade-In Options ........................................................................................ 54

The Much It Takes .................................................................. 55

## Chapter 13: How You Can Manage Risk in Options Trading ........................................................................................ 58

Use Your Trading Master Plan ............................................... 58

Using Option Spreads to Manage Risks ................................ 60

Risk Management Through Diversification ......................... 62

Risk Management Using Option Orders ............................................. 63
The Bottom Line ................................................................................ 64

**Chapter 14: How You Can Trade Options Intelligently ...... 65**

Exercise Active Learning ................................................................. 65
Consider the Key Elements in an Options Trade ........................... 66
   *Determining What Direction You Think the Stock Will Move* .. 66
   *Foresee How Low or High the Price of the Stock Will Move from Its Price at the Moment* ................................................................ 67
   *Predict the Time Frame Within Which the Stock Is Expected to Move* ............................................................................................... 68

**Chapter 15: Technical Analysis ............................................ 70**

Comprehending Technical Analysis ................................................ 70
How Technical Analysis Can Help Traders .................................... 71
Using Charts in Technical Analysis ................................................. 72
Technical Analysis Indicators .......................................................... 73
Limitations of Technical Analysis ................................................... 74

**Chapter 16: The Supports and Resistances ....................... 76**

**Chapter 17: The Main Features of Technical Analysis ........ 81**

**Chapter 18: The Different Types of Graphs that Exist in Technical Analysis ............................................................. 86**

Line Charts ....................................................................................... 87
Bar Graphs (OHLC) ......................................................................... 88
Candle Sticks Charts ....................................................................... 89

**Chapter 19: The Possible Advantages of Applying Technical Analysis ................................................................................ 91**

Provision of Current Information ................................................... 91
Depicts the Trend of Price Movements .......................................... 92
Depiction of History ........................................................................ 93
Timing Provision .............................................................................. 94

Provision to Be Used in Any Market.................................................95

**Chapter 20: The Strategies and Tricks That Can Be Applied with Technical Analysis........................................................96**

    Steps to The Strategies Used in Analyzing Options........................ 98

        Identification of a Technical Analysis Strategy..........................98

        Identification of Tradable Options That Fit with the Technical Strategy ................................................................................................99

        Finding of a Brokerage Account for Existing Trades ................99

        Selection of a Good Interface to Track and Monitor Trade.....100

        Identification of Other Applications That Can be Implemented on the Settled Strategy ........................................................................100

**Chapter 21: How to Control Emotions: Have a Right Mental Approach ............................................................................................. 101**

    Steps to Help Improve Your Trading Psychology..........................103

**Chapter 22: The Basics of Psychology in Trading ............ 106**

    Challenges of Trading..........................................................................107

    Emotional Trading................................................................................108

    Greed .........................................................................................................109

**Chapter 23: Why Those with the Right Mindset Become Successful Traders........................................................................ 111**

**Chapter 24: Mistakes to Avoid on the Expiration Day ...... 115**

**Chapter 25: Other Strategies for Beginners in Option Trading ................................................................................................ 120**

    Long Straddle Strategy ................................................................... 121

    Buy-Write Strategy ..........................................................................122

    Married Put Strategy .......................................................................122

    Protective Collar Strategy..............................................................123

    Long Strangle Strategy ...................................................................124

**Chapter 26: The Best Strategies to Invest with Call and Put Options Trading............................................................................... 125**

**Chapter 27: Describe Examples of Trade ............................ 130**

    Position Trading .................................................................. 131

    Day Trading ........................................................................ 131

    Scalping ............................................................................... 132

    Momentum Trading ............................................................ 133

    Swing Trading ..................................................................... 133

**Chapter 28. Probable Tips and Suggestions to Try to Succeed with Options Trading ........................................................ 135**

**Chapter 29: Possible Errors to Avoid That Can Be Committed in Option Trading ............................................................. 140**

    Buying into the Option of the Out-Of-The-Money Call Options ... 141

    Lack of a Strategy in Trading .............................................. 141

    Lack of a Strategy in Exiting the Market ............................ 141

    Not Putting into Consideration, the Expiry Date ............... 142

    Having so Much Leverage on the Trades Made ................ 142

    Trading with the Less Expensive Options ......................... 143

    Indecision on Early Options ............................................... 143

    Trading with the Wrong Size of a Trade ............................ 144

    Maximizing on a Losing Trade ........................................... 144

    Trading in Options That Are Not Liquid ........................... 145

**Chapter 30: The Conclusion on What Was Written and the Goodness of the Book ...................................................... 146**

**Description ........................................................................ 150**

# Chapter 1: The Basics of Options Trading

When you hear about investment what clicks right away for most people is stocks and bonds. The word options trading escapes unnoticed.

An option is a contract allowing the bearer (but not forcing the bearer) to either put or call the stated asset at a named price within a defined period of time. A call option allows the bearer to buy stock while a put option allows the bearer to sell the stock.

Investors' portfolios are usually made up with a number of asset classes. It could be stocks, currencies, bonds, ETFs or cash equivalents. Another type of asset class is options and when used in an appropriate manner they offer more advantages than stocks and ETFs combined.

Options can positively affect an individual's portfolio through added income, protection and leverage depending on the situation. Another use is that they help in speculation purposes.

Options are a member of a group of securities called derivatives. From the perspective that, the price of options is dependent on the going price of other assets. Derivatives may include things like; futures, forwards, mortgage-backed securities, calls, and swaps.

Being an asset option can be purchased like any other asset. An investor needs a brokerage account to invest in the stocks they hope will turn their initial investment into a lifetime fortune.

It is important to find a broker that gives you access to all the kinds of different investments that are important to you. The key features to look in a good broker include;

- Low commissions
- Good research
- Great customer report

Options are best traded in the following platforms;

- **E*TRADE**
  Best for options overall
  E*TRADE offers quite expensive options trades but the magnitude held by this platform is great for options trading and the broker offers different mobile applications.

- **InteractiveBrokers- Lowest commissions**
  InteractiveBrokers is not the best platform for relaxed or unplanned individuals but it propels the industry in international trading and minimum commissions desired by more planned and informed traders.

- **TD Ameritrade- Best option tools**
  The increased expenditure incurred when trading with TD Ameritrade does not go unaccounted for. The brokerage offers amazing platforms, research, mobile apps, education, and customer inquiries. No doubt it has the top-bar grade in all-round experience.

- **TradeStation- Well-rounded offering**
  TradeStation is a well-established trading technology and it is very supportive of its web-based platform and active traders through its awarding desktop platform.

- **Charles Schwab- Unique order types**
  Talk about reduced costs, proper research, top-notch trade tools, and well-calculated future plans Charles Schwab will not let you down.

So how much do you need to have in your pocket to start this great investment journey?

Normally options trade in share blocks of 100, so a $1 option costs $100, commissions included. But also, options may be agreed on in any kind of named assets such as bonds, currencies or even commodities.

The upper hand in buying options is that an investor can take part in predicting the price moves of stock, without having liquid cash. Options trading is an almost high-risk area of the investment world. According to statistics conducted by CBOE just about 10% of options are carried out, 60% are closed out, and 30% goes to waste.

Where a broker is involved you should be notified that options never miss risks and are not for just anyone to venture in. Options trading is unpredictable and has a high-risk percentage of loss. The investor must be made aware of this before jumping into it.

Stocks and bonds have one thing in common with options and that is risks. Options trading takes more effort to do well than stock trading but it pays at the end of the game.

# Chapter 2: The Types of Options Trading

The financial market has lots of ways of making money. Options trading happens to be one of these methods. Like any other money-making scheme, there is always a need for a prior understanding of the dynamics of the trade in the spotlight. Stock markets have their own ways and regulations. To fit in you have to align with the trade that favors you and feels right. The main types of options trade are calls and puts. They don't stop there, they can also be classified on the basis of time a contract can be put to work, expiration date, the security they are connected to and lastly the method of trade. Discussed are the various types of options trades to top up the option trade knowledge.

Calls are those financial contracts; agreements that offer the owner mandate to purchase an underlying asset in the future at a price that was agreed on. Buyers of these options will do so with speculation that the price of the security will go higher. They identify a time when the value of the option is high enough and make a sale which comes with a profit. Sometimes daring before the exercise date can get you more than what the market price was, so patience may help earn more cash. These buyers of options can also be referred to as holders while those that assist them in selling the options are called writers.

The underlying security is said to be the asset that holds the contract. An example would be you purchase a call based on some shares in this company Y, by purchasing them you obtain the powers to buy shares in the same company. A call has an expiration date and therefore it has to be sold off at a profit before or on the expiry date. Sellers in a call option have the obligation to sell off the stocks as long as they are assigned.

Put options are the trade whereby you make a purchase on the rights to make a sale on all stocks at a better price at any moment before the set and agreed on the date of expiry. The price is predetermined. Inputs, the holders believe the stock price will decrease with time. The sellers of a put option find themselves in a spot where they are obligated to buy the stock if only, they are assigned. You will buy a put I you believe that its price will fall. Puts are therefore perfect tools for leverage and also important as hedging; reducing any risks predictable at a reasonable cost, tool in financial markets. Puts mean that if by example you buy a put based stock, it comes with the right to make sales on shares in the given company at a price; strike price. The strike price is the price that an options trade can be exercised on.

American style options have no relations to where the contracts are to be bought or sold. Its focus is on the terms agreeable on a contract. A normal put or call contract requires the buyer (put options) or the seller (call option) to exercise their securities at that time before the expiration date. In the American style option, the owner who owns the contract has some privileges that include a right to exercise at any given moment as long as its time prior to the expiration date. It is however not mandatory to follow the expiry date as a holder. This type of trade has some risks that it poses to the option sellers.

A European style option has a close similarity to the American one only that they differ at the time of exercise of the trade. With the European style of option trading, you can only exercise the right to buy; if it's a call option, or sell; if it's a put option on the exact date of expiration and not any time before or after. This style is advantageous because it is less common which translates to lower cost of maintaining it and running it. This type of trade also does not focus on geographical regions. This trade type has reduced flexibility that can be noted since it has also an effect on the contracts and tends to make them even cheaper.

Exchange-traded options are common around the globe. An exchange-traded option is commonly known as a listed option and it's a standardized form of the option. It can be sold or bought by just anyone interested in the trade but under the guidance and help of a broker sometimes. This group of trade type holds any option contract that is listed on a public trade exchange.

Over the counter option is another type of options trading that focuses on the purchase and sale of options only on the OTC markets; over the counter. They are well-tailored and have a bunch of complicated terms than most contracts. They are not readily available to the general public. It is also known as dealers' option since it involves two private parties that come up with their well-customized contract to accommodate the needs of the parties involved.

Apart from those discussed, types of options can also be based on the underlying securities. You would not believe me if I told you there are, many underlying securities available in the market. They include the following.

Stock options stand for those contracts in the form of shares that are available in a specific company that is already publicly listed.

Index options use the index in place of stocks as the underlying security.

Currency options involve grants to the ownership rights to place a purchase and sale that particular currency at a rate of exchange that was agreed earlier on.

Futures options include futures contracts. They give the owner the right to exercise and enter into a futures contract.

Commodity options involve physical commodities or commodity futures contracts as the underlying assets.

Basket options involve a contract that is based on a number of securities that have the potential to make to stocks, currencies and other financial instruments.

Options can also be categorized along with a timeframe. They can be regular, weekly, quarterly, and long term expiration anticipation securities.

# Chapter 3: The Advantages of Trading in Options

There are several people who have found it appealing to trade in stocks because of its popularity. This is because several people fear trading other financial instruments. This is not supposed to be the case since other financial instruments such as options have a myriad advantage in the financial markets. Despite several people trading stocks, the numbers of people who are trading options have increased tremendously over the years. The major trigger of this increase is the advantages possessed by options. These advantages include;

## Capital Outlay and Cost Efficiency

There is one of the major reasons that is owned by the trading of options. The talked about reason is the potential of making huge amounts of profits. It is more advantageous because an individual does not need to have huge capital investment in the trade. This phenomenon has made it ideal for an investor to focus on options trading because they can be able to start small as they invest more as time goes by. It is an attraction to even investors who have huge budgets as well because it proves to be cost-effective. In simple terms, one can be able to use leverage so as to acquire more trading power.

It is an occurrence has been proved to be true in the financial market. It is in the sense that an option trader can be able to purchase options of similar stock. This will give him or her the power to purchase the stock by using a call option. Buying options and later buy shares, in the event he or she sells the shares in the present market situation, one can be in a position to make a huge amount of profits. The trade of options has certain positions an individual can take to make sure that he or she save his or her capita investment depending on the underlying asset.

## Risk and Reward

The risk to reward advantage is often linked to the first advantage illustrated above. It is all narrows down to profits an individual is able to create in the options market. Traders and investors in the options markets are able to make proportionate gains with regards to the amount they have invested in the trade. A good depiction can be made from the potential an individual has to gunner from small investment which also has the potential of multiplying. The advantaged risk to reward ratio is achieved to its maximum potentials in the event that an individual uses the right strategies.

It is important for an individual to constantly note that there will always be risks involved in options trading. This is because it is a characteristic of any form of investment or business done by any person. There are trading strategies that can be very risky when it comes to using them to base critical decisions such as those that are speculative. The general rule in options trading is that speculation with high potential returns tends to have high-risk involvement in it. On the other hand, options that have low-risk levels tend to have fewer amounts of gains. Options trading involves various types of options contracts. This makes it easy for an individual to limit risks in option trading depending on the contract he or she has settled on.

# Flexibility and Versatility

Flexibility is one of the most appealing elements that options trading poses. It is often in contract to several forms that are resented as a passive investment while some are inactive forms. The common characterization here is that an individual is limited to making money or using other strategies. A good depiction can be used by an individual who buys stocks for the thought of building his or her portfolio so as to serve long term gains. Such an individual can be able to use two kinds of strategies. The first strategy will involve a trader focusing on the long term gains and purchasing a stock that has the potential to increase in value in the future. The second strategy will involve an options trader can choose to invest in stock that gives regular returns. Buy and hold is a strategy that has several techniques involved to help it to be a success.

However, the flexibility and versatility offered by the trading of options mean that an option trader has the potential of opening more opportunities. This means that a trader or investor of options has the ability to make profits in any kind of market condition. One is able to speculate price movements of foreign currencies, indices, and commodities. What this means is that a range of option trading strategies plays higher roles to a trader in the identification of other profitable ventures and being successful in them.

# Chapter 4: The Components of an Option Contract

## Underlying Asset

An underlying asset can be described as the financial assets in which prices of a derivative are based upon. In this case, the derivative will be options. It is a financial instrument that can price a specific asset. A good elucidation can be depicted by an option on a certain stock say XYZ. An options trader has the right to either sell or buy the option at an agreed strike option price which has a limited time. An underlying asset is able to spot the item being the aim of the contract. This helps an individual to be able to value the contract he or she is signing up for. The underlying asset tends to give participants of the security that is needed by both parties.

The price of the contract an individual is participating in is often determined by the type of asset being traded. The contract of an options trade is supposed to have two parties who are either buying or selling the underlying assets. Let's expound on the stock options as the underlying asset. If an individual has the potential of purchasing one hundred shares of a certain company at a price of one hundred American dollars, this will be the determinant of the value possessed by the option contract. An underlying asset can be a market index.

## Type of Trading Option

The current financial market has seen numerous types of options being traded. The contract agreed by option trading parties is supposed to have a clear indication of which type of option is being traded. The types of options that are known in the current world tend to categorize and named depending on the varied features they pose. People across the globe are familiar with two types of options. Calls and puts options are popular in the financial markets.

Puts option gives a trader the ability to sell underlying assets. On the other hand, call options give an individual trading option the right to purchase an underlying asset. There are two common types of options that have been featured in the options contracts are known as the American and European options. Entering into a contract of American options allows a financial trader to be able to trade his or her underlying assets between the date e or she had purchased them to the date they are bound to be invalid. On the other hand, trade options contracts that contain European options bound an individual to perform his or her trades on the edge of the expiry time.

## Strike Price

The presence of a strike price is a common phenomenon in the trade of options. It can be described as a major component when it narrows down to penning down of an option contract. Options such as calls and puts are heavily dependent on this factor. Its critical nature can be shown by an option trader who needs the call options. It is important because it determines the value possessed by the option. There are several people who have familiarized strike prices with a different name which is known as the exercise price.

The criticality of this component of the contract makes it one of the components that are discussed earlier between the contractual parties prior to them entering an agreement or contract. It is able to inform an investor or trader what the trader what in-the-value money is supposed to be achieved. The underlying price value of the traded assets is supposed to be lower than the strike price. In many cases, the strike price is always affected by the time frame of the contracts. One is supposed to remember that strike price operates on fixed amounts that can be converted to dollars. However, they vary depending on the contract and individual has.

## Premium Price

The premium can be described as the price an option buyer in a contract pays the seller of the option. Terms of an option contract state that the amount is always paid upfront. It is always important for a trader to always remember that this component of a contract is not refundable. The rule extends itself to the side that one cannot be refunded his or her money even if the contract has been exercised. The premium quotation in a contract is always done in a certain way for efficiency. The most common way across the globe entails the quotation of option in the foundation of shares which is termed per share basis. The amount of premium is always affected by several variables before it is agreed on. The common determinants of premium prices are swayed by three major factors that are the volatility value of the option price, its timing, and the intrinsic value.

## Expiration Date

One can easily understand the term expiration date of a contract as the last day he or she has the right to exercise either buying or selling the underlying financial instruments. A contract is termed worthless in moments the expiration date has passed. The expiration date tends to differ depending on the type of contract an individual has entered this despite the general principle of the contract being worthless after the last days. A contract using the American style of option trading gives an options trader the right to be able to trade his or her options from the date he or she purchased them to the day they expire. However, European sty trading fixes an individual to only performing his or her trades on the last days of contract expiration.

## Settlement Option

The settlement of options can be described as the process by which the holder and writer of an options contract resolve and exercise the terms stated. The process entails the participation of two parties in the trade of options and it differs depending on the options one has decided to trade. It can be illustrated with both the calls and puts options. In calls options, it involves a holder paying the writer of the option. This is the reverse in the puts options since the holder of the options is the one selling them.

# Chapter 5: The Fundamentals of the Pricing Options

Optional trading has grown significantly, even in the selling of stocks. The traders in this market care about the future growth of the business and not the present as opposed to the usual stock exchange. In this practice, one acquires the right to buy a stock but not the obligation. However, it should be before a certain maturation period. By the word obligation, it means that you are not mandated or forced to buy but is optional. This practice is a contract because it has the maturation period which the trader should follow.

You have to know the critical definition of some of the terms of this trading. These terms will prove significant in realizing the price trend of this trade. Remember that your main aim in the business is to have less value future contracts of buying an asset. You need to follow keenly on information regarding the assets to transact because their amount depends a lot on the premium you pay. The following are some of the terms found in this market.

There is a capped style option. This business is usually practiced when you are already aware of the asset's price. Therefore you can quickly evaluate the profit you will gain at the end of the maturation date. The risk of trading is also significantly reduced, and you can examine the right amount to use for the business.

Always remember that this business is related to forecasting of the future price and having the right to buy the assets with no obligation. However, you may wonder who facilitates such actions. It is not a broker as many of you may think but is an option writer. In simple, this person may be called the seller of an option. He or she is the mastermind of the whole process and will direct you on how to calculate the maturity value. The person also is in charge of receiving the premium. One extra thing with him is that he is obliged to buy the assets or the underlying security at the mandated price.

Sometimes due to the volatility of the market, you fear that the market will elapse significantly. There you make the right call by choosing the options trading. If you are that guy, who postpones the trading with the hope that it will maintain its worth at the expense of a volatile market, then you are wrong. Therefore, know that you are practicing the call options. This strategy is crucial if you anticipate that the market for the stocks is going to rise beyond your budget.

Another aspect is the put option which is vice versa of the call option. That involves the seller of the shares who fears that the stock market will recede. Therefore that seller will exercise the mandate to sell stocks at a particular price at a future date. In this case, the stock value falls below the next amount.

That future price is referred to as the strike price. It is thus the value that is realized at that scheduled times which the buyer or seller expects. More straightforward to say, is the value bought or sold over that specified period where you made either a call or put option. That price usually is exercised before the contract matures.

Everyone deserves the credit for their work even the option writer too. Therefore that credit is costly in terms of payments. You have to pay that individual an optional premium. That price is realized per the agreement between you and the optional writer. That right, you are buying or selling you have to secure it with the premiums paid. Otherwise, it will be reserved for somebody else.

You have to gauge the profit you will take in the optional trading. Therefore some terms like the intrinsic value should not escape your ears. This value is calculated by subtracting the value of the underlying stocks with the strike price. Remember that this trading is a derivative organ that depends on the amount of the fundamental asset. That fundamental has its market index, which must be less in case of call up or less in case of put up option.

Extrinsic value is another significant segment in this type of market. It is the value of that right against the intrinsic value. This trading is usually regarded as a time value fixture that has fewer profits.

## Assumptions and Consideration of Optional Pricing

One assumption is that the underlying price of the stock is evenly distributed. That means the logarithm in working on its value is constant. By doing so, you can anticipate what will be the strike value or the expected value of the assets. In other terms, the volatility and the trend of the market are specific. Recognize that the volatility is the sharp increase and decrease in the price of a stock. The scheme also makes the mathematical calculation of the premium and the intrinsic value operational because of that constant function.

There are no transaction costs realized in this avenue. Moreover, there are no taxes evaluated which are calculated alongside the striking value. Otherwise, the tax and transaction costs will influence the intrinsic value reached. Therefore by including those in the final value, there will be a sensitivity of the change in the financial instruments. Value relative to the price of the underlying assets.

There are no dividends too in this security. The bonus would operate just like the taxes and the transaction costs. That is to mean if they are included, the final value will be different from the expected. They too have to be paid per year, and it is practical to remove the dividends so that one can reach the accurate results.

The risks free rate is assumed as constant. This rate is typically associated with government subsidies or incentives. If these aspects were included, they would manipulate the results of the outcomes negatively.

Stock trading is also thought to be continuous. For you to oversee that future settlement of trade, it means that the securities will continue even at a next date. If the stocks were not continuous, then it would pose a threat to those traders with buying shares at future expectations.

# Chapter 6: How to Start Trading in Options

Would you agree that optional trading is exceptional? Some of you may not agree with this because you are fond of trading in the shares or the currencies which you consider less risky and volatile. How would you feel playing around with figure which future-oriented? Like a game of chess where you fill a puzzle of uncertainties, it is the same deal with optional trading where you do not know the future. Most of you discredit this trading because you think it is filled with uncertainties. However, with useful speculation of the trade, it will not earn you much of the risk. There are certain things you as the beginner you ought to follow. The following strategies to come up with the right option.

First is that you have to think of your investment objective. You do not go there in the trading aimlessly because you will lose a lot of money. Remember that options require that intelligent speculation because you are dealing with future gains. You have to establish realistic and measurable values that you expect. Such goals will give you a way to go and the route to follow. You may plan which type of optional trading you want. That is where you want the put off option or the call option. Moreover, do you want to speculate on the performance of the underlying asset or to hedge out their risks?

You have to examine the risks and the returns that the assets may bring you. Your biggest aim is always to harness sizeable gains while reducing the risks. You think that there are risks in the present and decide to buy them in the future. Or you with the put up option you predict that the shares will fall in the price and you award others right for protecting their expected depreciation. You have to be tolerant, optimistic, and persistent in your tasks. If you are a risk-taker, this is the right avenue for you. If you sense a volatile market exploit that opportunity to gain much.

Identify the different events of the market of the sector you are trading. Those events will institute the volatility of the occurrence. You can either experience a drift or a rise in the market. Those events can be grouped in two ways, where one is the market-wide, and the other is the stock specif. The market-wide are like those government jurisdictions that affect the economy of the whole sector. For example, the government banning or subsidizing some products. In the stock-specific one, they include issues like product launches and many others.

You have to derive the right strategies after knowing the stocks to trade and the returns you desire. These are distinctive tactics that you will apply to harness many gains. You must be that intelligent speculator who will read the patterns and try to realize the peak points and the volatility of the market. Moreover device some strategies like selling a call option against the stock. That is a tactic where you exercise a covered call approach on the security that you already own. You must sell the cover calls against your shares to identify the profitable spot. The other strategy is using the bullish or bearish strategy for call option and put option, respectively. Always buy puts options on significant stock platforms where you anticipate a substantial fallout of the top players in the industry.

Decide on the right parameter to facilitate your marketing. These are like the variables you will use to make a successful trading. Remember that for this trade, it requires one to know the trend, price analysis, and many other types.

## Steps of Optional Trading for a Beginner

First is to identify the right brokerage account. You can do that by researching those that pay well and with the right features. You can still seek recommendations from the expert dealers. Check on their websites and create an account by keying in your correct details. Therefore, try to log in where you should remember your password vividly.

When you log in to that platform, you will be asked to select the right trade options you want. By now you should know the firm you want to buy from which you choose. It depends on the brokerage account because you should click on the odder or trade platform after identifying the shares to buy. This page should be clearly labeled, where click on to go to the next phase.

Search for the specific stock you want to buy. If you cannot find it in the list of the many securities, search for it in the search box. There will be multiple displays of the live quotes of share that re being traded, hence select the one you want to buy. Still, you can navigate on the quote table to identify the primary and the options ones. Chose those alternatives because they are the reasons you are doing the trading.

Then there is the maturation month option where you must identify the peak times. That expiry period is the point where your contract ends; thus, you should set it according to your potential. The month should be realized when you have studied how the market behaves. You may have discovered that in a particular month the selling of shares is relatively high while in another period they are low. Choose that month that looks productive on your strike index.

Selecting your strike is the second last step. That is the amount of an asset in the predetermined period. It should level up to what you can afford and oversee if it generates good revenue. You should not set the illogical or unrealistic figure just because you want to earn more. Know your potential and the size of your wallet.

Select the put or call options that are found at different columns of the table. Usually, calls are grouped on the left and the puts on the right. Recognize the side you want to venture.

There is the platform for the quantity too. That is where you should fill the number of contracts you want to trade. Moreover set the price to pay for the option. Check and recheck the orders, when everything is clear now is right for you to confirm and send.

# Chapter 7: The Platforms and Tools for Trading Options

You can never choose the right brokerage firm until you are assured that it contains the essential features. Many firms like to be distinct and unique so that they can have that competitive edge against their competitors. There are many different styles of portraying the features of the options trading that includes even their standard trading program. Some platforms have gone as far as offering the customized accounts which feature your specific styles and features that you prefer.

It is upon you to research the trade wisely about which brokerage accounts that would suit you. Optional trading needs seriousness because you need to learn how the shares will fair even in the future time. There are also the tools necessary to facilitate this trading and interpretation in the trading. They also help you to analyze the mathematical concept of that particular business. Some of the platforms found in those brokerage accounts include the following

You may have been told severally by your elementary teacher that 'practice, practice makes perfect. The same concept needed here because you cannot wake up one early morning and find yourself professional in this trading. Therefore you have to exercise until you graduate from being an amateur to a professional trader. In that regard, some sites offer paper trade platforms. That is the accounts where there is fake cash. Remember that alternative trading is volatile where if you are an amateur, you can suffer quite big losses. However, the demo accounts will help you to prevent such misfortunes. You play around with these accounts because you are losing nothing in the game. You also gain experience in trading and identify the trend which you will use when you stake the actual payment. It also sharpens the skills of interpretation and analysis in trading. You have to be aggressive and consistently trading to gain that experience.

The technicalities of the trading deem you to sometimes search for a website where you engage other traders. Remember that you and other traders share the same interests, and you help each other to trade. For that concern, you establish a social networking platform for all traders. In simple, you are batching the networking program and compose all your marketing need to your audiences in social marketing. You first create a profile files with your status so that other people may know you. Then you make several posts to your friends who may help you in your trading scheme.

There is also risk management orders. What makes people fear most in optional trading is the volatility in the business. Therefore in the processing of hedging out any risks, you may realize that you have suffered substantial losses. However, you need to reduce such losses. You use this site to learn the risk control orders such as the stop loss ones. For that reason, be vigilant in the trading and do no fear the risks, that moment you fail to stake your cash maybe the moment destined for your success.

There is also a personalized or customized layout in the trading. Some of the features found in brokerage accounts must correspond to your individual needs. Some of these brokers will contact you to detail them on which layout you prefer. That in particular concerns with the type of charts, the variable to use, and how they should be arranged in the layout. You always feel psyched to trade on a platform that you prefer. You even believe your chances of amercing good returns in the optional accounts are increased.

# Which Are the Tools Known in the Optional Trading Is the Charts

The charts are some of the essential tools for optional binary trading. These charts are diagrams that exhibit trading schemes. They are featured with horizontal and vertical axis each with the independent and dependent variables respectively. In some firms, these charts are advanced in that they enable one to react to the fast-moving prices. They still have risk controller platforms. You have to analyze these charts to know how the options trade will fair. Recognize their marketing predictor's ability of the tables too. If you are an experienced reader, you will have just a glance at the chart and determine the trend the trade is following. Remember that you are making the future derivatives where the charts must also outline the value of the underlying assets and the staking price.

You need the indicators which show you the performance of the trading. This phenomenon shows you the direction and the trend of buying or selling. You also establish the volatile regions where the peak times and the recession point are also known. Check an indicator such as the MACD, where it measures the trend and the direction of the price. Here you quickly detect a high and a low trade.

The use of technical analysis tools is crucial in this subject because you will learn about the technicalities that make you succeed. This tool links the chart with the indicators. Is serves to predict the options trade price by checking at its past performance. Therefore you do not have to research for information on other sites or manuals. However, you can have that historical and trend data at the trading platform. By using this approach you can examine the type of indicators in measuring the trend. That is like the volume indicator which is located below the price pointer. It has a calibration like green and red. If the price moves upward, it is showed by green and if it moves down, it is shown by red.

Another technical analysis tool is the chart pattern. It mainly consists of the trend continuation patterns which shows that the correlation of the prices which are moving in the same direction. The trend reversal trend is another type in which its figures are moving in the opposite direction. Take an example of the rising wedge that is found in the trend continuation and the falling wedge in the reversal pattern. The one found in the rising contention has the bearish movement and the one falling has the bullish effect. Remember that for the bearish effect it is concerned with the put options and for the bullish is related to the call type. Therefore, these effects prompt the rising wedge to move in the same direction and the falling wedge moves in the opposite direction as you are operating with a call option.

# Chapter 8: Leverage

Leverage is a term that is, in most cases, made use in financial management. It comes up from borrowing capital as a way of funding as well as expanding an investment. It will then generate some returns on the risk capital. It is a strategy to invest in using money that is borrowed. It increases the profits of the investment made. Leverage can as well be the debt amount that a company puts in use to finance its assets. When the leverage is high, that means that the investor has more debt that has accumulated than the equity. Leverage is known to boost the returns and hence, an increase in the profit.

It multiplies the potential returns from a particular investment. It will bring down the is likely to come up in case the investment you have made does not turn out as you had expected. The idea of leverage is put I use by investors as well as firms. An investor will use to make sure that there is an increase in returns on the investment. The investment will be levered using specific instruments, including margin accounts, options as well as futures. Companies will use leverage to finance their assets. Instead of issuing stock so that they can raise capital, they decide to use the debt to finance, aiming to increase the shareholder value.

Investors do not prefer to use leverage in a direct way they have their means to access it indirectly. They opt to invest in a company that they know uses force to fund as well as expand their investments. The company does not have to increase the outlay necessarily. Leverage is an excellent approach anyone can put in use to multiply the buying power in the trade out there. However, you can decide to use margin as a way of creating leverage.

## Types of Leverages

There are several types of leverage, but they do not need to be combined with being productive. They instead form the entire process even though they are independent. They include;

## Operating Leverage

Operating leverage is just concerned with the investment activities of an individual firm. It is about the incurrence of the fixed cost of operation in a company's income stream. The operating price can either be fixed, semi-fixed, variable as well as semi-variable. The fixed fee is contractual, and it is subject to time. It does not necessarily have to change when the sales change, and it is supposed to be paid despite the number of sales.

Variable cost t has a direct variation with the level of sales revenue. There will be no variable cost if there will be no any sales that are made in a certain period. Semi-variable, as well as semi-fixed, will vary partly with the number of purchases made and it will remain partially fixed. It is subject to be broken down into variable as well as fixed portions and is brought together according to the variable or the fixed cost. The fixed operating cost can be subject to be put in a lever, and hence the decisions of investment will go in favor of using assets that have a fixed price.

When a firm decides to use the fixed cost, it will increase the effect that a change will have on the sales when EBIT changes. The ability that a firm will have to put the fixed operating cost in use to increase its earnings before the interest as well as the taxes is what is known as operating leverage. The leverage will be concerning the variation of the sales as well as profit. When the percentage of the operating cost is high, then there will be a rise in the level of operating cost.

## Financial Leverage

It is a relation to the combination of debts as well as equity in the capital format of a company. When there are financial charges in existence, the financial leverage will as well exist. The business costs should not depend on the operating profits in any way. The sources in which the funds that help to boost an investment come from can be put in categories. The funds can either be having a fixed charge, and some may not be having the fixed financial cost. Debentures, preference shares, bonds as well as long-term loans have a fixed financial burden. Equity shares are known to have no fixed charge at all.

The fixed financial charge is used as a lever, and hence, the business decisions will go in favor when you employ such funds. When there are fixed charges in a company's income stream, financial leverage will be an outcome. It is an excellent idea to make sure that the change that will be made in EBIT to affect EPS will be significant. The higher the level of fixed charges, the higher the probability that the degree of financial leverage will go up. When the fixed costs do down, the economic advantage will go down as well.

## Combined Leverage

If you bring both the operating leverage and the financial leverage together, they will come up with the combined force. It is concerning the risk of one not being able to cover up for the total amount of the fixed charges. When a firm can cover fully on the operating as well as the financial burdens that is when the term combined leverage comes in. The higher the fixed operating cost as well as the financial charges, the higher the level of the combined force.

## Working Capital Leverage

When there is a decrease in the investment of a particular asset, there will be an increase in profit. When there are many investors in the market and dealing with the same trade, there will be decreased profit. When there is a decrease in the investment of an asset, the risk associated with it will go high. That means that risks, as well as returns, have direct relations. When the probability of risk goes up, there is a likely hood that the profit will increase as well. The ability of an individual firm to increase the effect of the change in the current stock on the firm's returns is working capital leverage. It is so when there is an assumption that the liabilities are constant.

# Chapter 9: Why Leverage can be Riskier

At some point, you will need to take some loans so that you can expand your investment. Debt financing is attractive since the lending entity will not in any way dictate how you will use the credit. When a firm has a lot of pending debts in comparison with the operating cash as well as equity, it is highly leveraged. When a company's leverage is high, it, in turn, becomes sensitive to the economic changes. They too are subject to the risk of being bankrupt. The reason why leverage is riskier is that they are subject to;

## Limited Growth

When you have a loan, the lending company will expect that you will pay in the period that was agreed upon when you were getting the loan. They hope that you will be on time and no failures should come along the way. It is a problem when an investor borrows money for a long-term project that will not generate some income immediately. That will make them find an alternative to how they will pay the loan to avoid breaching the contract. If the payment period has come, and the investor has no returns, paying the mortgage can be a burden in one way or the other. When you decide to start paying the loan, it will mean that you use the money you borrowed to pay back. When that happens, you will have less money for financing your operations. You will not be in a position to implement full on the plan that you had. That means that you can have retardation, and you will not execute your plan fully. When investing, you need a plan and to set deadlines for the completion so that you will remain on your focus. When you have to pay the loan with the money that you borrowed, you will not be in a position to hit your deadlines. That will mean that you will experience limited growth, and you may not have the potential to continue as per the plan.

## Losing Assets

When you are unable to pay loans, and you are highly leveraged, that can lead to a conspirator of the assets that you have. There is no way that a company should pay capital sourcing from equity. When that happens, and the lender expects that you will pay your loan in time, they can decide to take some of your assets to stand in for the loan. The assets can be of a similar value or a value higher than your investment. When in a loan, the company is supposed to pay the lender before any other deductions. Repossession of assets can happen if there is no money to pay the lender in time. It the lender has to be paid even before the employees of the company, it means that the employees may look for another option and quit working with you. That will make you lose assets of value, and you will be left stranded.

## Inability to Get More Financing

Before a lender gives you money to invest in any trade, they will first check out whether you have any other loan. They will do that to establish how secure their payment is with you. If you are in debt, no lender will want to lend you more because they are not sure whether you will be in a position to clear their debt. They will access the risk that is associated in case the company goes down, meaning there will be no one to pay their loan. When a company goes down, it is declared bankrupt, and that means that the lender cannot claim their money even on a legal basis. No lender will agree to put them last on your loan list since they know they will be the last to be paid.

## An Investor Will Not Be in a Position to Attract Equity

When a company has high leverage, they are not able to increase the equity capital amount. And it is rare for an investor to give money to a business that has bid records of unclear loans. In the same way, lenders will avoid providing more money to a company with high amounts of investments, and the same way investors avoid such business. You will lose the potential of attracting investors when you have a lot of pending debts. When a lender knows they are the last in your line to be paid their loan, they will not find it comfortable to lend you. If at with any chance you get an investor to give you, they will demand a significant percentage in terms of ownership in return of borrowing you the money.

## Multiple as Well as Constant Losses

There is a risk in leverage in cases where you invest in a particular stock and the price of the stock takes a negative change when you least expect. You will end up suffering a lot of losses since you have to pay the loan back in time and you have other expenses to deduct. That will be hard on you since there is no profit made considering you made a loss. Taking a loan can begin with the increase in losses as well as end with the losses locking in within a short period. High amounts of debts can get out of hand and can lead to bankruptcy at a very high speed. When you are declared bankrupt, it comes with several consequences. There is no time that you will get any other loan no matter how you will have an enticing business plan. No investor will want to have an association with a bankrupt person. That will make any investor who has the potential to fund you to pull out.

Even though you need a lot of money to invest in a long-term plan, you need to have an idea of how to repay the loan. The project you have May not at times work in the way you would want it to and the need to have a back-up plan. If it is necessary, avoid late payment of loans and maintain the discipline of the highest level when the repayment period arrives. If you observe all the rules layout when taking the loan, you will not have a hard time with the lender. They will be willing to lend you more and more when you need it.

# Chapter 10: The Advantage of Trading with Leverage

In trading, one opts for premises or rather a transaction that is profit-generating and one that plays a critical role in increasing the capital base of an investor. In other words, no one enters into any trade to suffer a loss. However, individuals, as well as premises, take time to think of the options that will help them solidify a marketing position and earn more profits in the long run. In Forex trading, the decision that one takes plays a critical role in determining whether one will earn profits or not. However, taking leverage options might be the best decision that one can make. Even though force is associated with several risks, it has the benefits that it carries as well. As outlined earlier, the higher the risk, the higher the probability of getting high profits. The advantages of trading with leverage include and not limited to. Take a look at some of the advantages of leverage options:

## Increase in Profit

Leverage will earn you more benefits without necessarily having to put in more effort. Since it is borrowed money, you do not have to toil so much so that you can earn it; instead, you look for a lender. When you fulfill the requirements, the lender will finance you and you will have to repay back when the period lapses. When you inject more capital into a business, it is likely to give you more returns under favorable market conditions. It does not matter the amount that you are adding to the investment. You can stake a large or a small amount and your profits will not remain at the same level they were before you get the loan. It does not matter the kind of trade that you are in; what matters is that you have added more capital in it. There will be an overall growth when more financing is put in a business, meaning that there will be growing as well in the levels of profit. Leverage makes sure that you are one step ahead all the time and a step forward in terms of profit.

When you need to inject more capital into a business, the primary objective is to make more money out of it. That is why people go for leverage since there is no other way to raise funds in a fast way. When you take a loan, you need to have a commitment in the business you are doing and invest your time is that it will have positive yields. When you take a loan, and you forget about being zealous, you will suffer losses and the need to be active. Let your focus be to multiply the money is that you can get some to pay the loan with interest and you can achieve your aim for making a profit. Before you go for the loan, take a scan of the trade you want to invest in, and see the changes it has to make more money. Pick on the hot deal, and you will have good returns at the end of the day.

## An Increase in Capital Efficiency

When you increase the amount of money in a particular transaction can lead to a rise in productivity on how you use your capital. You need to consider capital as an asset, and it can increase the level of yields. When you take a loan, you will increase the amount of money, and you will raise the level of efficiency. The amount you get when there is no loan in your trade will mean that it will rise when you add more capital. Reinvesting more times will make sure that more frequency, as well as efficiency, is arrived at. Leverage will not just increase the profit level, and it will as well give a considerable return on the investment within a short period.

## Is a Tool that Mitigates Against Low Volatility

Leverage is a great approach that can be put in place to mitigate the effect brought about by low volatility. Volatile trade is known to deliver huge profits in the Forex trade. It can deliver good benefits from a small transaction and can shield against the effect that comes with low volatility. A small entity can become a big firm with the help of leverage. Leverage will help you to capitalize on the small significant levels of movement in the trading price.

Leverage is double-edged, and it will work for you in a great way. When things turn around you, it will be hard to get out of such a position. And so, the need to be extra careful when you are dealing with leverage since it can be a rescue tool for an investment that is going under. It is an alternative that you can seek when you need to boost your trade. When you are choosing leverage, choose the one that is in line with the trading strategy you have. Do not take much loan than you need since it will give you a hard time when repaying, and maybe you did not invest all in the business. You will struggle when paying, and no return is seen.

## Low Cost of Entry

The arithmetic options that are used in leverage options are relatively cheap, but the resultant profits are relatively high. In other words, one is required to pay a relatively small amount to fit in the market. You can buy as low as 50 shares with a minimum of $1000. It is worth noting that the option is simple, but there are many chances of getting higher profits. The aspect is critical in the sense that the number of risks involved is relatively low than the benefits accrued to this option. The other element that makes it more straightforward is the fact that it is one of the most flexible options. Traders are given several options that allow them to earn well despite having used a minimal amount of capital used as the initial investment.

# Chapter 11: The Disadvantages of Trading Leverage Options

## Lower Liquidity

It is worth noting that a lot of individual stock options dint has many volumes. There are cases where one is forced to own very few stocks. The aspect that in all the options that one has will trade at different strikes of payments as well as expectations, the particular option will be forced to have a less volume unless it is one of the most popular stock index or stocks. However, the lower liquidity won't affect smaller traders who would prefer working with manageable amounts of about ten contacts. Larger traders with more than 100 contracts will be forced to have other options or undergo an extra cost to increase their volume. Some are forced to take several options to compensate for fewer amounts. However, there are cases where such an opportunity doesn't work due to the rules and regulations that operate in different organizations. In most cases, the traders are forced to accept the lower volume and look for other options of investing. However, the art of being forced to take only the popular options or rather the stock indexes that have larger volumes causes them to suffer a massive loss in case the organizations fail to meet its target.

## High Spreads

The art of lacking liquidity among these trading options causes higher spreads. The aspect is detrimental due to the fact that one is forced to pay more indirect costs while using thus trade option. The element is linked to the fact that when one is using the opportunity, they will be spreading the trade. It is worth noting that larger organizations of firms with higher operations power are forced to pay more indirect costs to compensate for this spread. The aspect becomes a fail when issues crop up, and the firm is forced to limit the art of range.

In most cases, individual or rather organizations which had primarily invested in the premises are forced to suffer huge losses as the organizations look for ways of compensation. It is worth noting that there are cases where the firms with large contracts are forced to outline all the options of trade and use all of them as a means of compensating for the low liquidity. The art increases the spread, and more risks are attracted. The aspect is linked to the fact that the owner or the organization will have to pay all the indirect costs to compensate for the many spreads.

## Higher Commissions

When one is operating with such organizations, one is forced to pay using commission terms. In other words, one has to pay a certain amount of commission for each dollar that is invested. The demerit is worsened by the fact that the option has very many options that forced one to have a lot of spreads. It is worth noting that for all the ranges that one is involved in, there is a certain amount of commission that one has to pay. The aspect is detrimental since the organization has low liquidity and attracts from more spreads. Thus, in case of any loss, the premises or rather individuals who have invested using such an option are forced to dig deeper in their pockets so as they can compensate for the commission required to fund or allow such possibilities of trade to be operational.

## Complicated

One of the aspects that forced people or instead traders to ignore the options of trade in the fact that it is one of the most difficult choices. There comes a time where even those who have been investing with the option, fail to understand the processing of their trade. The aspect is more complicated among beginners. In other words, beginners fail to know the number of options they ought to take before they can think of investing. There are numerous cases where traders are confused about the number of spreads to be involved in. The other option that complicates everything is the fact that one has to pay in terms of commission. The aspect is challenging as these commissions aren't fixed. In other words, they keep changing from time to time. It is worth noting that the art of having complicated options causes traders to opt for other options that seem natural and command higher profits in the long run.

## Time Decay

When you buy this option, one is forced to lose the value of time and money. In other words, as you hold these options, you lose their value in terms of time. The more you keep them, the more you lose their value. One of the most difficult and challenging aspects of this option is that there is no exception over this rule. In other words, so long as you take this opportunity, you will have to hold it for some time. The more you keep, the worse it becomes as their value reduces.

## Less Information

The option is very painful when one is forced to accept whatever they receive. In other words, there are no options where one is given the complete information of what is happening with their accounts. In most cases, the choices don't provide analytical information about the organization. What happens is that the owners try to understand what they receive with the mind that their options lost their value as they were holding them.

## Availability

It is worth noting that this option is not available for all the stocks. In other words, although the option is available for several shares, there are still limits over the capital that applies the option. The aspect is more complicated as one may not comprehend the kind of stock that takes this option. The limitation is detrimental in the sense that it puts the traders in jeopardy over the opportunity to choose. The aspect is linked to the fact that few options have such terms. In most cases, one is forced to consult brokers who end up charging other fees hence increasing the commissions that one has to pay for the option.

# Chapter 12: How Much Leverage It Takes to Trade-In Options

Leveraging options can be compelling when it comes to the art of investing. In other words, if the season works out in the best way for you, you will enjoy the fruits of the option. The aspect is linked to the fact that the number of commissions might reduce as well as the expenses and the profits earned might rise with immeasurable value. There are cases where small amounts of capital are invested using this trade option, and in the long run, the premises earn a lot of profits. The profits earned are then channeled to the various traders who opted to take the leverage option. When one is having different financial instruments such as stock, one may take advantage of the possibilities and borrow funds that take the position forever. In other words, with such devices, the art of investing using leverage options becomes available. One of the best choices about this contract is the fact that the leverage option contracts them. The aspect causes a great multiplication that increases the amount that one had invested.

# The Much It Takes

When one is buying contracts, one is allowed to control more considerable amounts of underlying security such as stock. The aspect is critical in the sense that such options trade by themselves. In other words, one doesn't have to be in the market and do the trading. However, the option contracts the leverage themselves and multiplies the amount of capital that was initially invested. In the long run, more profits are generated to the winners in these accounts. In other words, if you have some capital and want to invest using these options, you can buy a stock that uses leverage and earn in the long run.

For instance, if you wanted to invest $ 1000and wish to use a company that is well known in the nation. One of the aspects that emerge from such an option is that you expect the organization to increase the investment and turn it into a profit-making opportunity. However, this is not what happens always. There are situations where the organization misses the mark and loses are channeled to the owners of these options. If the organization or rather the company of choice trade its shares $20, you will be forced to buy at least 50 shares with your $1000 investment. In case the organization does well in terms of its operation, and a profit is generated, the shares will be sold at a higher price. For instance, if the shares trade at $25 each, when all the shares are resold, the owner of the option will earn $5 in each stock and amass a profit of about $250.

When it comes to leverage option, let's assume you want to invest $1000 in the same company trading at $2 with a strike price of about $20. If the contract size is, let's say 100, you will be in a position of buying five contracts at $200 each. The aspect means that you will be in a good option of controlling over 500 shared in the organization. The element is different from the first option, where one is forced to buy only 50 shares directly. In other words, leverage options provide opportunities for taking contracts instead of buying shares directly from the organization. In the long run, a lot of profits are generated to the owners of the leverage option.

The aspect illustrates the basic principle of how leverage works. One of the merits of the leverage option is that it can command a lot of funds or instead profits with very little starting capital. In most cases, the organization or stock with leverage options encourages even small traders who might be having a small amount of money, to begin with. However, with time and with a favorite season, the organization can generate a lot of profits that are in turn made to the owners of these options.

Thus, one can earn as much as they can invest. In other words, the amount received depends on the option that one takes, as well as the funds spent. However, with as low as $100, one can enter into a few contacts with the origination offering the option at a relatively low price. The aspect is critical in the sense that the organization does well, and it doesn't depend on the possibilities one had taken. All the profits are channeled to the owners of these leverage options depending on the number of contracts that one had.

It is worth noting that the price option that one takes moves as a fraction of the entire amount. The other aspect worth noting is that if you have a choice of $5, it is not a must that the earning be $5 more. Depending on the opportunity as well as the season of the organization, one can command higher or fewer profits. The aspect depends on the calculations as well as the commissions that one is forced to pay. However, in most cases, individuals, as well as an organization, can command higher profits, and there are cases where their ama9unt of investment doubles. The aspect indicates that there are no limits over what you can earn provided the organization is generating profits and channeling them your way.

In a nutshell, the ability to use leverage to multiply the profits is a massive advantage to various trading options. In other words, with the right timing and the best trading options, organizations, as well as traders, can earn a lot of profits. However, increased earning attracts several risks on the premises. Thus, before you opt over any investment plan or instead leverage option, it is wise to consider the options available as well as the risks therein. The aspect is linked to the fact that you may earn a lot of profits but end up suffering losses due to the risks involved. It is wise to be aware of the role of money in your leverage contact.

# Chapter 13: How You Can Manage Risk in Options Trading

Appropriate risk management in options trading may sound like an outdated idea to some people but the truth is that effective risk management is the number one recipe for success in options trading. Being able to efficiently manage your risk exposure as well as your capital is key when trading options. In as much as risk is basically unavoidable in any business venture, the exposure to risk should not be a problem. The key solution is to take measures that will successfully manage the finances that are at risk. Always make sure that you consent to the degree of risk you are exposing your trade to and that you do not expose yourself to untenable loses.

In this chapter, we take a look at some of the measures you can put in place to manage your risk exposure.

## Use Your Trading Master Plan

It is crucial to be in possession of a comprehensive trading master plan that designs the parameters as well as guidelines for the trade. The most practical uses of this kind of plan include money management and most importantly, in this case, managing your exposure to risk. Your trading plan should be inclusive of detailed information on the degree of risk that you are at ease with as well as the amount of capital you intend to invest with.

When you follow your plan to the letter and strictly use the funds that have been categorically set aside for the purpose of options trading, it becomes easy to fend off some of the greatest blunders that traders and investors make, such as, investing using funds that are "scared".

The moment you opt to trade using finances that you should have allocated to other uses or finances that you simply cannot afford to divest, chances are that you will not make logical decisions in your trading activities. Whereas it is hard to entirely do away with emotions that come forth in options trading, you desperately need to focus as much as possible on your trading activities. Why?

As soon as emotions overwhelm you, chances are that you will begin losing your focus and consequently behave in an irrational manner. For example, you can be driven to carry out transactions that you would otherwise not have made in normal circumstances. However, if you strictly work in accordance with the design of your trading plan and strictly use the resources you allocated to investment, then chances are that you will take control of your emotions.

You should also strictly abide by the degree of risk that is stated in the trading plan. Giving your consent to trades that are low risk means that you should refrain from putting yourself in positions that will expose you to higher risks. Usually, it is tempting to put yourself in vulnerable positions by exposing yourself to risk if you make a couple of losses and yet you are in the quest to make things right, or perhaps you have performed exceptionally well with a number of low-risk trades and you have the desire to revamp your gains at a much quicker faster. If your choice was to settle for minimal risk investment, there is definitely no need to go out of your safe zone by falling prey to the emotions we discussed earlier on.

## Using Option Spreads to Manage Risks

Option spreads can be termed as powerful and necessary instruments whenever you are trading in options. Options spreads are basically whenever you integrate more than one position on options agreements in reference to similar fundamental security to efficiently come up with a general position of trade.

An example would be, making a purchase in the money calls on a certain stock then going ahead to write out of money calls that are cheaper on that stock. Doing this means that you will have come up with a type of spread that is usually referred to as the bull spread. Purchasing calls insinuates that you are in a position to make gains if the value of the basic stock upsurges. However, you will lose a section of or all the funds used to purchase them if it happens that the stock's price failed to rise. When you opt to write calls based on that same stock, you will have the ability to take control of a number of costs you incurred initially and consequently cut down the total amount of funds you could have lost.

Virtually all the strategies of options trading call for spreads to be used and these spreads are a representation of a very efficient way to mitigate risk. They can also be used to cut down the upfront costs of getting into a position and lessening the number of finances you are in a position to lose, just like in the bull spread example we have discussed above. This basically means that you probably cut down the profits you should have made but eventually managing the general risk.

Spreads are equally important when somebody seeks to reduce the risks that come whenever you enter a position that is short. It is possible to get into positions that present you with a chance to gain profits if the prices move in your favor, however, you can effectively minimize any losses you would have incurred if the movement of prices did not favor you. This explains why very many options traders use spreads; they are magnificent tools for risk management.

There is a wide range of spreads that have the ability to take control of virtually any condition that the market brings forth.

# Risk Management Through Diversification

Being diversified is an instrument used to manage risks by traders who are creating a collection of stocks through a strategy of buying and holding. The underlying criterion of being diversified for this kind of traders is the dissemination of trades to a range of different sectors and companies and building up a portfolio that is balanced instead of having a lot of funds stacked up together in one sector or company. A portfolio that is diversified is broadly considered to have minimal exposure to risk in comparison to a portfolio that is composed of mainly one particular kind of investment.

In matters related to options trading, being diversified is not really important in a manner similar to the one discussed above. Nonetheless, it still has a variety of uses that you can use to carry out diversification in a number of dissimilar ways. In as much as the principle mostly remains unchanged, you should not have a lot of capital tied to one specific type of investment.

Diversification can be carried out using selected and varying strategies by executing trading options that are dependent on a series of fundamental securities, as well as ensuring that you trade in a variety of options. Basically, the goal behind being diversified is that you have the potential to make profits in different ways and that you do not completely rely on one specific outcome for the success of all your trading ventures.

# Risk Management Using Option Orders

A comparatively easy way to mitigate risk is to make use of the various orders that you have the potential to place. To add to the four key order types that are used in close and open positions, there are a series of extra orders that can be placed, and the majority of these can be instrumental in managing risks.

For instance, a normal order in the market will be completely full upon the availability of the finest price during risk implementation. It is an excellently basic method of selling as well as buying options, however, in turbulent markets, chances are that your order might get full at either lower or higher price than how you expected it turn out.

In addition, there are orders that can be used in making the process of exiting a position automatically. This is irrespective of whether it aims at locking in profit that has been made or cutting losses on trading activities whose outcomes were not favorable. Making use of orders like the trailing stop order or market stop order, you acquire the ability to easily determine the point to leave a position.

This process will be crucial in helping you avoid situations where you do not get profits because you stuck in one position for a relatively long period of time or suffer losses because you did not close out on an unfavorable position fast enough. When you use option orders in the right way, you can minimize the risk you get exposed to any time you trade.

# The Bottom Line

Very many people who are new to the field of options trading make a gruesome mistake of blindly investing a lot of their money in their business ventures. This exposes them to a series of risks, including the loss of significant amounts of hard-earned money. Therefore, determining the right amount of funds to use as capita and how to use it in options trading gives the investor the ability to unlock the potential of leverage. The main solution to handling being exposed to risk is to ask yourself a number of "what if" questions, and as you do so make sure that you use risk tolerance as the guiding factor.

# Chapter 14: How You Can Trade Options Intelligently

Even with its numerous benefits, options trading exposes the trader to the risk of losing their capital, and it is known to be naturally speculative. Not everybody has the ability to become an intelligent options trader. This is because smart options trading requires a trader to have a specific set of skills, attitude as well as personality type.

Here, we will discuss some of the ways you can trade-in options intelligently.

## Exercise Active Learning

A report from the Chicago board of trade indicated that 90% of traders who venture into options trading incur significant losses. What barricades the intelligent traders from the average ones is that smart options traders ensure that they learn from their misdoings and consequently the lessons they acquire in their trading strategies. Smart options traders have practiced, and practiced even more over time until they fully understood the lessons behind every loss they incurred, they grasped the economics that steers the market, as well as how the market behaves on different occasions.

Financial markets are in a state of continuous change and evolution; a smart trader has to clearly comprehend what is taking place and how the entire system works. By exercising active learning, you will not only have the ability to execute your current strategies but you will equally have the ability to spot opportunities that other people may bypass or not see.

## Consider the Key Elements in an Options Trade

When you decide to take out an option, you are acquiring a contract to sell or buy a stock, normally one hundred shares of the stock for every contract, at a pre-arranged price by a given date. You must make three critical choices before you place the trade:

## Determining What Direction You Think the Stock Will Move

This greatly affects the kind of options contract you adopt. If you feel like the stock prices will go up, you will choose to buy a call option. A call option refers to a contract that allows you to buy but does not obligate you to purchase a stock at a prearranged price (usually referred to as the strike price) in a given period.

If you are of the idea that the price of stocks will decrease you will purchase a put option. This kind of option allows you but does not obligate you to trade in shares at a stated amount of money before the expiry of the contract.

## Foresee How Low or High the Price of the Stock Will Move from Its Price at the Moment

It is advisable to purchase an option that will show where you expect the stock will be located during the lifetime of the option.

For instance, if you feel like the price of shares of a company that is presently trading at $100 will go up to $ 120 sometime in the future, you will purchase a call option that has a price that is lower than $120. In this scenario, you will hypothetically opt for a strike price that is not greater than $120 subtracted from the option's cost, in that the option still rakes in profits at $120. If it happens that the stock actually rises beyond the strike price, then your option is in the funds.

In the same way, if you are of the belief that the share price of the company will go down to $80, you would opt to purchase a put option (allowing you to sell shares) at a strike price that is higher than $80 (preferably a strike price that is not below $80 in addition to the option's cost in such a way that the option still rakes in profit at $80). If the stock dips under the strike price, your option lies in the money.

It is important to note that you cannot just choose whichever strike price you want. Option quotes, professionally referred to as option chains have a variety of strike prices within easy reach. The accretion in the midst of strike prices are regulated throughout the industry and usually depend on the price of the stock.

The amount that you pay for an option, usually referred to as the premium, contains two elements: time value and intrinsic value. Time Value refers to whatever remains, and it includes how turbulent the stock is, interest rates, the time left before it expires among other components. On the other hand, intrinsic value refers to the disparity between the share price and the strike price, on condition that the stock price is higher than that of the strike. For instance, let us say you have a call option worth $100 whereas the price of the stocks is $110. Let us make an assumption that the option is at a premium of $15. Ths time value will be $5 whereas the intrinsic value amounts to $10 ($110 subtracted from 100).

## Predict the Time Frame Within Which the Stock Is Expected to Move

All the options contract that you purchase have an expiry date that shows the final day you can use the option. It is also important to note that in this case, you cannot simply generate a date out of nowhere. The choice of a date is determined by the ones that are given whenever you bring forward an options chain.

Expiry dates range from years to months or even days. Weekly and daily options have a tendency to be extremely risky and are set aside for experienced traders. For investors who have been in the trade for a long time, annual and monthly expiry dates are preferred. prolonged dates of expiry give the stock ample time to move and wait for your investment proposition to play out.

A prolonged expiry date is also important because it gives the option enough time to add value, regardless of whether the prices of stocks is lower than the strike price. The time value of an option decays as the expiry date comes closer, and option purchasers do not desire to see the options they bought reduce in value, possibly expiring without any value if the stock turns out to be below the strike price at the end of the period.

# Chapter 15: Technical Analysis

Technical analysis is increasingly becoming a favored viewpoint to trading, gratitude in part to the development in trading platforms as well as charting package. Nonetheless, a new trader comprehending technical analysis as well as how it can assist in foreseeing market trends can be challenging and daunting.

Technical analysis basically involves studying the manner in which prices move within a market, in such a way that traders use patterns from historic charts and indicators to foresee the impending market trends. It is a visual reflection of the present and past performance of a given market and it enables traders to make use of this information in the fashion of indicators, patterns, as well as price action, inform and guide forthcoming trends before getting into a trade.

Here, we focus on the basics of technical analysis and consequently how it can be put into use in trading.

## Comprehending Technical Analysis

The technical analysis mainly involves interpreting patterns in charts. Traders use historic data that solely depends on volume and price and consequently use the information they acquire to spot lucrative opportunities to trade based on familiar or habitual patterns in the market. Charts are exposed to a variety of indicators to establish points of entry and exit to enable traders to maximize the potential of a trade at a ratio of good risk to rewards.

In as much as the people who support fundamental analysis have a belief that economic factor mainly contributes to market movements, technical analysis traders insist that olden trends are helpful in foreseeing price movements in the future. In as much as these styles of trade vary, comprehending the disparity between technical and fundamental analysis as well as how to collaborate them can be very advantageous in the long run.

## How Technical Analysis Can Help Traders

Numerous trades have approved technical analysis as an instrument for managing risks, which can be a major setback. As soon as a trader comprehends the principles and concepts of technical analysis, he/she can use it in virtually any market, thus making it an adjustable analytical instrument. As fundamental analysis seeks to identify a market's intrinsic value, the technical analysis seeks to spot trends that can suitably be caused by basic fundamentals.

- Technical analysis has the following benefits:
- It can be used as an independent method.
- It is applicable to any market using any timespan.

- Technical analysis enables traders to spot patterns in the market.

## Using Charts in Technical Analysis

Technical analysis is centered around charts. This is simply because the only way to gauge a market's past and current performance is by analysis the price; this is where you kick off the process of analyzing the ability of a trade. It is possible to represent price action on a chart because it is the most uncensorable indicator of the impacts of the price.

Charts are useful in finding the general trend, regardless of whether there is a downward or upward trend over a short or long term or to discover rage bound circumstances. The most known types of technical analysis charts include candlestick charts, line charts, and bar charts.

Whenever you use a bar or candlestick chart, every period will feed the technical analyst with information on the high and low of the period, the price where it started and also the close. Candlestick analysis is preferable the patterns as well as how they are interconnected can help in predicting the direction of the price in the future.

As soon as a trader comprehends the fundamentals of charting, they can use indicators to help in predicting the trend.

# Technical Analysis Indicators

Technical traders use indicators whenever they are looking for windows of opportunity in the market. In as much as there are very many indicators, price, and volume-based indicators. These are useful in finding out the levels of resistance and support are, how they are breached or maintained as well as determining how long a trend is.

A trader has the ability to see the price as well as any other indicator by doing an analysis of numerous time frames ranging from a second to a month. This, in turn, gives the trader a different view of the price action.

The most known indicators in regard to technical analysis are:

- The corresponding strength indexes
- Moving averages
- Moving average divergence as well convergence

The last two indicators in the list above are usually used to spot market trends whereas the corresponding strength index is basically employed in finding out probable points of exit and entry. Indicators help traders in conducting an analysis of the market, finding entry points and doing validation of how trades have been set up.

# Limitations of Technical Analysis

The major setback to the authenticity of technical analysis is the economic aspect of the efficient markets hypothesis (EMH). EMH asserts that market prices are a reflection of all past and current information, therefore, there is no way to exploit mispricing or patterns to get more profits. Fundamental analysts and economists who have a belief in efficient markets have no belief that any sort of information that can be acted on is contained in volume data and historical price, and in addition, that history does not repeat itself, instead, prices shift like an unplanned walk.

Technical analysis is also under criticism because it is applicable in some cases only because it contains a self-actualization prophecy. For instance, most traders will position their order to stop loss under the two-hundred-day motion average of a given company. Considering that a variety of traders have done that and it happens that the stock gets to this price, then the number of sell orders will be enormous and it will shove the stock downwards, approving the movement that traders were anticipating.

Thereafter, other traders will notice the reduction in price and also opt to put their positions up for sale, consequently improving the robustness of the trend. This selling pressure that is generally short-term can be regarded as self-fulfilling, however, it will have very minimal direction on where the price of assets will be a couple of weeks or months to come. To sum it up, if people employ similar signals, it could result in movements foreseen by the signal, but eventually, this main group of traders become incapable of steering price.

# Chapter 16: The Supports and Resistances

The chart patterns in any kind of trade calls for support and resistance. Whether you are dealing with fired trading, commodities, stocks, futures or options. In any world of trading, it is the basis of the chart patterns. To understand better what support and resistance mean in the options trade, you can relate to the most common type of trade that is easily accessed by almost everyone because everyone is involved in at least one type of trade in the market.

Let's take an example of a situation where you go to the market to purchase a commodity that you've been using frequently. In this case, you are the bull. This is a product that you like so much and to encourage the seller to restock this product, there's that price that you will support so hard that you don't want it to fall. This is what we refer to as 'Support.' The buyer takes control of the prices and protects it so that it doesn't go down. The reason as to why the buyer would want to prevent the price from going down to the extreme is because of the fear that the seller would stop bringing the commodity on the market because they won't see its value. This is the concept of support that can be easily understood by anyone.

For resistance, it's the other way round. Here the seller now takes control of the price and prevents it from rising higher. For trading to carry on successfully, the buyer and the seller must agree on a specific price. Raising the price too high may make the bull to reconsider an alternative commodity with a lower price depending on the amount of money they would want to spend. On the other hand, the seller would not consider trading at an extremely lower price than what they expect. This is because no one easily accepts a loss. Selling at weird spoils the motive that someone had for participating in the market.

Investors trade depending on the price levels. For instance, someone would prefer to purchase a good when the price of commodities is at a level where it is more likely to shoot after some time. When it happens as per their expectations, then it's a favor on their side because they are going to record again when they resell the commodity. This level where a large number of investors tend to believe that the prices will rise higher is what is known as the support level. It is what determines the decisions made by the majority of investors. When a support level is broken, it changes its worth and becomes the new resistance level.

At the resistance level, the investors always assume that the prices will fall lower. This makes the major investors think otherwise. Those who purchase commodities in bulk when the price is lower and is expected to move higher would not want to proceed to purchase the same commodity when they know that the price is more likely to drop so low that if they go ahead and sell it at that price, they would record a huge loss. Also, when the resistance level is broken, it changes and becomes the new support level.

On many occasions in the market, you will realize what is referred to as 'Noise'. This is when there are errors in pricing making them go beyond limits. The tops and bases of pricing are exceeded which may lead to misunderstanding between the bulls and the bears. However, this is a normal activity in the market and the traders always take care of it to ensure that trade moves on, even though it always brings some disagreements in most cases.

Beginner traders must always understand the concept of support and resistance to enable them to trade successfully without having diverted minds on what they are doing. When they get to understand how the market prices fluctuate with different seasons, they will be in a position to decide which commodity to trade with during what season. The errors associated with market pricing should be clearly understood by the beginner trades to prevent them from getting stranded when the price levels change from time to time.

Someone who is new to the trading market is sometimes made to believe that when the commodity prices are low, they are definitely meant to rise higher after some time and this is where they normally get disappointed when the prices fall lower. It is normal that the prices go extremely down and this is always assumed to occur when new goods arrive in the market and replace the old ones. Many people would prefer going for the latest commodity instead of the previous one.

Buyers and sellers must always come to an agreement for the prices of every commodity. This is because the investors' plans are always different from the plans of any other normal trader. Understanding the level prices is not always easy for beginner traders but once they get used to it, trading becomes easy for them and they find it more comfortable dealing with different clients. Maintaining support levels and resistance levels helps both the bulls and bears to maintain good trading relationship and remain positive about the results of the trade.

A good support level encourages the investors to invest more in the commodity with the belief that when they will be exchanging this particular commodity at a later date, the market prices will be fair on their side making them earn a reasonable profit. At this time, the previous buyer now becomes the seller and they have the task of controlling the prices of goods to ensure that it doesn't rise higher making it difficult for others to purchase. Everyone has a different preference when it comes to trading. Setting a higher resistance level can sometimes make it difficult for the seller to earn the expected profit. This normally happens when the buyers shift to a lower price commodity and let go of yours because it is not affordable to them. This only leads to you

# Chapter 17: The Main Features of Technical Analysis

Technical analysis of options trading always shows how successful options trading has become and what normally leads to its success. It lists the number of successful trade on the option and what contributed to the success of these traders. Definitely, there are guides and trading techniques that a trader should always consider for them to achieve success. The analysis of options trade has always shown different features and the main feature we are going to discuss below.

First and foremost, we are going to talk about discipline. This is the key to any successful trade or even a project. As a trader, you need to be highly disciplined about what you are doing. It is however not so easy being disciplined up to a certain point in options trading but still for you to be successful, you must always exercise discipline in your field. You need to be highly committed to what you are doing for you to achieve the best that you need. You don't necessarily have to concentrate on one thing the whole day but the commitment that you show is very important.

You also need to learn from the losses that you encountered in the past. It is normal for all traders to record a loss at some point during the trading session. This does not mean that trading should stop. You learn from the loss, pick up and move on. No shortcut. You should be in a position to accept the losses and carry on with trade because of everyone's losses and if everyone was to panic and quit there would be no trading that would be proceeding until success is recorded. If you trade, lose and give up, there is no progress.

You should also be ready to learn. You are new in the market and you don't have a full idea about what you are doing. You just allow yourself to take lessons from the experts and be ready to apply the same tactics for you to carry on successfully. Watch what others do. How they carry out trade and respond to different matters is very important. You will realize you are gaining more and being well prepared to go for what you want. Technical analysis shows that if you are not well experienced in the field of options trading, you are only subjected to making mire errors than you work to succeed.

Be the decision-maker in your trading. Don't wait for others to decide for you what to do. Being your own decision maker allows you to carry out your trade successfully without putting blames on anyone. Learning for yourself is very important as much as you feel you need to take lessons from what is happening where you are. Nothing should influence you and dictate the decisions that you make. Take lessons but be independent in selecting what is best for you. This is the only way you can keep moving forward. Following what someone else is doing only leads you to a destination that was never meant for you.

A trading plan is another important feature of technical analysis of options trading. You should always have a trading plan of your own. Plan yourself well and decide what is best for you. You know exactly what you can handle and what you cannot handle and this means if you let someone plan for you, you risk straining to do something that is not within your level capacity. This only makes trading boring for you and that's why most traders quit and divert their attention to something else or blame someone for making them fail.

Watch how you react. Don't just react because you are supposed to react. The careless reaction is the number one cause of failure in any world of trading. You may face losses in your trade or some difficulties that come unplanned. How you react to them is what is more important. How do you handle losses? How do you respond to your client when something is not right? Being proactive helps you build good customer relationship with your clients and also help you to remain positive to keep moving on despite the challenges. Understand the market and making decisions based on your trading plans. Letting emotions take over you and control how you react will only interfere with how you participate in the market.

Develop a broad scope of learning. Don't just stick to one idea and think you are good to go. Everything needs a wide view so that you know how to attack everything from a different angle. When you have more ideas on what you are doing, you will find it easy switching to another plan when one fails. Being in a position to have several options helps you as a trader to be at room temperature with all types of trades. Open up your mind to convince different ideas in different fields.

Do not be in a hurry. Everything needs time so be patient. Take your time to balance ideas before you come to a final decision. Analyze every plan you have carefully and know the possible results of every decision you make. This will help you when it comes to arriving at safe decisions. Any decision made in a hurry has always led to the failure of most traders. Rushed decisions are always a result of panic so be relaxed and follow your trade plans carefully.

Lay aside your ego. Nothing can be successful if the ego takes the center stage. Avoid unnecessary ego and open up your mind to work with your clients at their level. Be ready to listen to them and deliver according to their interests. Your interests are not your client's interests and it is important to note that. Putting your ego before everything will only push away clients painting you a failure. For you to be successful, you have to let go of your ego and remain humble and respectful throughout the business session.

Having the above features in your mind and putting each of them to practice is what will move you to the next level. Play safe.

# Chapter 18: The Different Types of Graphs that Exist in Technical Analysis

Graphs that are used to analyze technical analysis are commonly referred to as charts. The technical analysis charts that are used in the financial markets tend to aim in identification two major components in trading. They narrow down to depicting the trends and patterns that are being experienced in foreign exchange markets. There are other chart functions that are used in the process of an individual trying to understand the financial markets. It can be a hard task to interpret the graphs for an individual who is a beginner in the financial markets.

There several forms of graphs that are used in the current world to analyze financial markets technically. However, there are three common graphs that are heavily relied on by traders in this sector of trading. These charts include candlesticks, line charts, and graphs. There is a common similarity that is shared across the three graphs. They are all created by the use of the same price data. However, the difference crops in when it comes to it come to displaying of data. All three graphs have a different way in which they display the data.

The difference between the three major types of graphs makes a trader have varied forms of technical analysis. However, the graphs have various advantages that they present to a trader investing his or her time and resources in financial markets. They help a trader to make informed decisions about the market. The advantages and uses of technical analysis graphs can be effectively used in the trade of options. These analyzing graphs include;

## Line Charts

This form of type of graphs is common in financial markets. It is common for people who are known for trading stock. However, the fame and advantage of this analysis graph have led it to be used in the trade of options. It this sector of financial trading, it has proved to also be effective in the roles it is tasked with. People who are beginners in options trading and other forms of financial trading are always encouraged to use this graph because one can easily understand it. It is easy for someone to interpret this graph because it focuses on the market holistically. This helps to eliminate the shifts in data that proves to be a heavy task for various people. Emotions are always put aside because this form of analysis uses factual figures presented to it.

What this graph simply does is illustrating the display are the closing prices. There is nothing else that is portrayed in the line charts. Each of the portrayed closing prices tends to be linked to the closing price that was seen in the previous trading session. This makes a continuous line that flows easily. This type of graph has places that easily depict it. They are popular in several web articles, newspapers and television programs. It is because they can be easily digested by several people. The graph provides an individual with less amount of information to handle. This is completely different from those bar charts or candlesticks. One can describe the graph as having a simplistic view of the market with just a simple glance.

There is something intriguing when it comes to the advantage of this graph helping an individual to manage his or her emotions. The process of trading is done by humans who are characterized by having feelings attached to what they do. These emotions are drawn away by the usage of neutral colors. Several choppy movements have easily eliminated the usage of several colors

## Bar Graphs (OHLC)

Individuals who commonly trade options that involve commodities as the underlying assets are commonly known to use this graph. It is very popular because of its effectiveness in the financial markets and its success is vastly experienced in trading stock options and foreign exchange markets. An individual who is at the intermediate level of options trading will be advantaged to using this graph while studying the market. There is a unique way by which this graph analyses the trends in the market. The data collected on the prices of financial instruments help to sport the trend in the market. They help in the identification of the entry and support or resistance points in the trade of options. The advantage with this graph is it's detailed hence giving added information to a trader.

This bar graph is able to display closing, opening, high and low prices for specific periods that are designated in the bar. The high and low prices in the graph create the vertical line of the graph. There are always two dashes that are present in the graph. The one of the left always signifies the signals of closings price while the one on the right signifies the signals of opening prices. There is a similarity that is presented between this kind of graph and candlestick. Both graphs are easily viewed on the sides though the bar graph tends to have a clearer view.

## Candle Sticks Charts

There are individuals who are used to trade in the financial markets tend to use this graph to analyze the options markets. They can be equated to the bar graphs since they are commonly preferred by intermediate traders in the trade of options. Candlestick can look easier in a trader's eye compared to bar graphs because of their full nature.

A candlestick graph does a function of displaying the opening, closing (OHLC), low and high prices in the for the period that is designated for each candle. The candle body of each stick represents the opening and closing prices. On the other side, the candle wicks tend to signify the high and low prices for each specific period. There are several colors that are used in this graph which are green and red. The green color represents the prices closing high than when they were opened. On another hand, the red color signifies the prices closed low than when they were opened.

# Chapter 19: The Possible Advantages of Applying Technical Analysis

There are several advantages that are accompanied by the usage of technical analysis. The most common users of these forms of analysis are the short term traders. It has seen a success story in markets such as options trading. These advantages include;

## Provision of Current Information

The current price tends to reflect the present information about a specific price of an asset. There are certain moments that rumors have the potential of consistently swirling the price causing a surge in the market. However, a balancing point is always achieved when the current price is depicted in the markets. The options market is characterized by the movement of traders and investors swaying most of the time. These two groups of a participant in the financial market can sway to becoming buyers or sellers. This situation occurs through the speculation of the value of the option being traded.

There are moments during trading that a tricky situation can present itself. Traders and investors tend to rely on the price charts because of a solid reason. It is because the charts tend to contain all perceptions and information about the value of an option or other underlying assets. The used information about an asset's value is recorded in charts using the gyration form. A trader in the financial market tends not to concentrate on why prices irrespective of if they rise or fall. This is despite them being able to show a trader when buying interests in more than selling interests and vice versa.

This has the potential of making trading of options to be much simpler to several participants. It is because the technical analysis focuses on the price charts. It is easy because an individual does not have to spend much of his time reading the latest financial news or analyzing the financial statements.

## Depicts the Trend of Price Movements

There are moments that traders can have a difficult time to make gains in the financial markets. One of these moments is when the prices of options are gyrating. During the moments of wild gyrations, the overall prices of options tend to sway greatly with the experienced trends. Directional bias is a common occurrence which proves to be advantageous to several traders in the financial markets. There are several ways that technical analysis proves its wits on this issue. It is able to determine when the market trend is in place when is not being experienced and moments it is reversing.

Strategies that use the trend to base their trading methods tend to be very profitable. There is a common way that individuals can use technical analysis to achieve this phenomenon. An options trader begins by first by isolating the trend. He or she then goes ahead to finding the viable opportunities that are going in the same direction as the current market trends. This helps an options trader to be able to capitalize on the price movements that are biased. There are various degrees that this trend can occur. The upward trend can go on for several weeks or days which are accurately depicted in the charts. The downtrends are always depicted on the left side of the charts.

## Depiction of History

Technical analysis is hugely based on unearthing the common patterns that are seen day in day out during options trading. These patterns are used several times in options after being uncovered by traders. However, one is not supposed to be brainwashed by this kind of reasoning. It is because one is prone to thinking that history is bound to repeating itself. A good depiction of this advantage possessed by technical analysis is portrayed by the chart known as the triangle. The common constructs tend to be similar, however; there are moments the constructed triangle can either be larger or smaller than the initial triangle. It means that the results can be able to pop out differently from the prior construct thus the odds of history repeating itself has very low odds.

One is supposed to realize what the essence of human psychology plays in this case. It is prone to not shifting most of the time. Technical analysis is prone to revealing that that options market is commonly characterized by several rise and fall in price value of options. Therefore, an individual is able to know how to deal with emotions of greed and fear when they are triggered during the process of trading. Emotions can also be patterned by the use of technical analysis when it comes to the values of the underlying financial assets. The history depicted by these factors plays a crucial role in making a major decision in the market since they act as a bearing.

## Timing Provision

Technical analysis has time provision as one of its major advantages. It provides an options trader with accurate timing of his or her trades in the financial markets. There are several findings an individual can be able to dig out in moments he or she uses the fundamental approach as his or her strategy. The findings can make individual trading options to speculate of gains in the value of options that are being traded. However, this is not the same case that a trader using technical analysis will be subjected to. A technical analyst is able to find leverage of waiting till the prices are able to inform him or her that the prices of options are about to rise.

## Provision to Be Used in Any Market

The concept of technical analysis can be used to variedly numerous fields. This has seen its application in several markets such as binary options, stocks, forex, futures, and CDFs. The pattern of human psychology and market trends has a high potential of being depicted in several markets. There are several moments this knowledge can be useful to an options trader. It is because; some options can be used to trade other underlying financial assets. These moments can prove to be the best points in trade and options trader can use this concept.

# Chapter 20: The Strategies and Tricks That Can Be Applied with Technical Analysis

Several investors in the finical market are known for analyzing options they own based on the fundamentals they possess. This includes looking at an option's valuation and revenue. However, fundamentals have low odds when it narrows down to portraying the current market prices of options as the underlying financial assets. It is where technical analysis comes to save an options trader in the financial markets. It is because it is it helps an individual to maneuver through the gap that is created between market prices and the intrinsic value of options. The action is made to be simple because of fundamental analysis has a way of leveraging behavioral economics and statistical analysis. This has seen the rise of numbers in traders and investors using technical analysis.

There are major approaches that are used by participants of options trading when it comes to technical analysis. These major approaches are two and they include a top-down approach and bottom-up technical forms. The top-down approach has several traders who prefer it. Most of the traders that are characterized by using the top-down approach in the options market are the short term traders. The long-term trader and investors are prone to using the bottom-up approach because it favors them.

- **Top-Down Approach**; it involves an options trader or investor screening for particular options. The intended options are supposed to be able to fit certain forms of stocks that fit the intended criteria. A good depiction can be sourced from a trader looking from options that have their moving averages at fifty days.
- **Bottom-Up Approach**; this entails an options trader analyzing options that have an appearance that is fundamentally interesting. These stocks tend to give an individual an added advantage in knowing the exit and entry points in the trade of options. An easy illustration can be used for those options that have a downtrend. With the use of technical analysis, a trader in the options trading can be able to identify entry and exit points. These points are critical in moments the options are swaying in the market.

The current world has millions of options traders who prefer to use different forms of technical analysis. Options traders who perform day trading tend to prefer simple volume and trade indicators in moments they make trading decisions. On the other hand, swing traders tend to have a preferential of using the chart patterns and other technical indicators. The trade of options has seen several technological advancements in it. It has to lead to several traders developing algorithms that are highly automated. They tend to anchor their analysis on volume and technical indicators to base their decisions in the options markets.

## Steps to The Strategies Used in Analyzing Options

There are five steps that are core in realizing the strategies used to analyzing options using technical analysis. These steps include;

## Identification of a Technical Analysis Strategy

This is the first step and it can also be referred to as the development of a trading system. We can use a situation of a beginner in this case who is participating in the options market. He or she is supposed to follow the strategy that involves the usage of moving averages. The option trader is supposed to track two moving averages in a specific option market. The two moving averages can be those of fifty or two hundred days. The fifty-day moving average can be used for the basis of supporting the short term trading options. On the other hand, options traders aiming for the long term trading of options can use the two hundred moving averages. A buying signal is always portrayed when the trends in a price move upward while the signal of trader to sell his or her options is realized in moments the prices of options have a downward trend.

## Identification of Tradable Options That Fit with the Technical Strategy

The common knowledge in option trading is that not all kinds of options have similar strategies that are applied to them. Most of the techniques stated above tend to favor options that are highly gyrating in nature than those that are not volatile. This case might favor the usage of moving averages that are characterized by fifty days. However, an individual can use the two hundred days if the option he or she is trading is not volatile in the options market.

## Finding of a Brokerage Account for Existing Trades

An options trader is supposed to be in apposition that he or she has found the right brokerage account to be able to conduct his or her trade. The account is supposed to have a certain minimum requirement for its success. An account used by a trader in options trading is supposed to be an able function to the utmost best in being able to track and monitor the technical tools used in technical analysis. A good account is supposed to do this function with the reduction of costs involved in accessing this data. One will be on a very good side of options trading if his or her account can be able to incorporate candlesticks.

## Selection of a Good Interface to Track and Monitor Trade

Options traders can differ on the level of functionality which is dependent on the functionality of the strategy he or she is using. A good depiction can be made of a trader who requires a margin account that provides information about the market. On the other hand, several people prefer basic accounts because they have low-cost options in them.

## Identification of Other Applications That Can be Implemented on the Settled Strategy

There might be other options that might need extra happening for a trader to realize maximum gains from them. There are options traders who have gone to the extent of receiving mobile notifications about any changes that can be experienced in the options markets. There are options traders who have automated their accounts to an extent they perform automated functions for them.

# Chapter 21: How to Control Emotions: Have a Right Mental Approach

When most people start trading, they are so eager to make money, and most of their decisions are emotional. Instead of being strategic and strictly follow their plan, they rely on their emotions to make trade decisions. Often, a trader will find himself making pushing trades when it's not the right time in the market to trade. Other times, due to motions, the trader will make losses without making stops and even take profits too soon in fear that waiting for the profits might result in losing it. Most of these emotions come when a trader thinks that they are missing profits easily made by other traders. In the eagerness to catch up, they will end up making emotional decisions instead of following through their plans.

The solution to avoid emotion trading is to start treating the trading market seriously, even if you are trading for yourself. Treat the trading as if it was your own business by creating a business plan with achievable goals and a daily routine. By doing this, you are sure that you have your emotions to the side, and you are now doing the business with the right mental state. What a business plan is to help a trader remove any sorts of emotion greed that may come long and also eliminate the emotions of fear. It also helps a trader stop forcing trade whenever they are feeling bored or even when they are going through the internal pressure of production.

Understanding trading psychology, therefore, becomes very important so that a trader is able to separate emotions from trading. Psychology involves understanding the mind and behavior that follows; in this case, therefore, we are trying to understand how the mind is involved in the trade. Trading involves controlling the figures, but controlling the trader's emotions is what will lead to reasonable control of the statistics. Some traders may argue that there is no way emotions are involved in trading, but there are so many losses that happen every day, not because of bad traders. It is because good traders let emotions get in their way of good trading judgment. The decisions made out of emotions quite often ignore the basics of trading and do not follow a trader's trading plan. The end result for a trader who lets emotions take over is never good. Therefore a trader having the right mindset free of emotions is what trading psychology is all about.

Trading psychology helps a trader reduce mistakes made on the impulsive judgment. The trader learns how to assess his reactions when trading and therefore, able to identify emotions that could help him to make bad decisions. Usually, bad decisions are a result of fear after losing trade severally. A trader will then react by holding on to a position for so long expecting things to make a turnaround. But a trader who is in their right state of mind knows that by doing the hold-up, it will result in further loss and it is always a great idea to close the position.

## Steps to Help Improve Your Trading Psychology

- Setting your mind right and freeing yourself from emotional trading is only achievable if a trader is continuously motivating himself. Encourage yourself to accept the fact that you do not need to pressure yourself too much. That other trader's success does not need to give you panic attacks. The trader needs to allow himself time to grow on his own and learn from the mistakes. Allowing fear to take over is what will cost a trader and make him trade from emotions of another failure. Every day before starting a trade, the trader should take time to meditate on the day ahead. This will make him more mentally prepared for all the risks and challenges ahead of you. When the mind is mentally prepared, the trader gets calmness and therefore eliminates the possibilities of quick emotional decisions. Meditating on the day helps you reduce all types of emotions that may affect your performance. Plus you have already allowed yourself time to accept that if any loss occurs during the day, it won't change your trading life.

- Another way to control your emotions is by increasing your overall knowledge of the market. When you are knowledgeable about what you are expected to do, you will not be afraid of taking risks. When you know what to do as a trader, you will rely on your knowledge rather than your emotions to make decisions. No matter how much tempted you to feel to follow your emotions or what an emotional trader would call instincts, you will do what is right. Being knowledgeable means that you know how much every decision counts, and therefore, you will try to get rid of the emotions. Knowledge about the market gives you some sense of calmness that you need to make decisions. Without calmness, it means you are making decisions without clearly thinking about the consequences. Patience allows you to think ahead in terms of what you can do when faced with all the market risks.

- As a trader, sometimes your emotions will tell you that you are not good enough and that you will make losses. Start allowing positive emotions by thinking of how strong you are. When you think of yourself as someone who can achieve anything, you will win the day. Thinking of yourself positively will help you always see the bigger picture at all times, and you will feel more encouraged. Positivity eliminates negative emotions.

- It's also important to think of what failing would mean to you. This will motivate you to do the best you can to eliminate emotions that may lead you to that failure.

- Remind yourself always what will be at stake if you allow negative emotions to take over you. Think of how much you stand to lose should you make decisions based on your emotions.

- Observe what other traders do because sometimes you continue making the same mistakes because your guts fail you. There is always something to borrow from others that will help you make better trading judgments.

- The best way to boost your emotions is to look back at your journey. This will encourage you to keep pushing on when you see the achievements you have made and also how the failures made you strong.

# Chapter 22: The Basics of Psychology in Trading

Despite the many risks involved in trading, people don't seem to give up on entering and staying in the market. The chances of loss in this market are so high, and many traders have lost so much money. However, for the traders that have achieved, trading is by far the most rewarding way to make money. Trading gives trader independence because they do not need to be employed anymore; they can employ themselves as traders. It also provides a person with a financial breakthrough if their trading works for them. Trading is like having your business, and therefore you become a sole proprietor, managing your own money and time.

# Challenges of Trading

There are so many challenges involved in the market for a trader, especially for the newcomers in the market. For this reason, not many people are able to stick around the market for long. When a trader lasts long, it is usually an expensive experience for the trader. Statistics show that not many traders continue in the market for more than four weeks for short-term traders. While for long-term traders, not many people make it past five years. This is quite shocking that a trader would put money in an investment and opt-out after a month. However, it is not impossible in trading because trading can be expensive. It is costly because if you put too much money into the trade and lose it all within the first month, you are unlikely to have the will to add more money. The entering capital can also be very expensive because to make a lot of profits you need a substantial capital. However, small capital can also produce significant profits, but it takes a lot of time that most traders are unwilling to wait on. Someone may want quick money, and trading is not the place for fast cash, you need a lot of patience. Therefore for a person who is the breadwinner, it becomes hard to wait until the earnings start feeding the family. However, with patience and a lot of practice and significant decisions in trading, trade is the most fulfilling career.

## Emotional Trading

A trader's psychological behavior has a lot to do with their success or losses. Being able to handle your emotions as a trader is what will determine your achievements in the market. Every decision needs-controlled emotion because failure to that the decisions will be wrong and damaging for the trader. The two most damaging emotions involved in trading include fear of failure and greed to overachieve. When a trader allows these two emotions to take over his trading experiences, he is unlikely to make it for long in the market. Therefore, these two need to be handled with care because they are emotions in every human being, and they do not necessarily need to eliminate but to be controlled. The following is an outlook of how the two emotions affect a trader.

Fear or panic – Fear is reasonable; it makes a trader careful about making bad decisions that could lead him to lose significant in the market. Fear in trading, when done in the right state of mind, can lead to great success because you will use that emotion to help prevent you from making hasty or delayed decisions in trade. Fear can be looked at in two different ways to distinguish the right kind and the wrong kind.

Fear of failing- This type of fear is when a trader is continuously worrying about a possible loss in the trading market because they feel that failure will define them. For this reason, a trader will always put himself under pressure to perform because they do not want to lose. Any sign of an upcoming loss will throw them off balance to the point that they will make a rushed decision to avoid it.

Fear of succeeding- this type of fear involves a trade being so afraid to make it significant that they let opportunities slide away from them. A trader will have the right opportunity to make a close that could be his great blessing but will be afraid to do so because he is afraid he is not ready for that kind of success. The trader will, therefore, wait for things to come a little down before making a close.

When fear is involved when making trades, a trader is likely to have panic attacks and also be extremely stressed. Stress will make a trader very exhausted that they will not enjoy the trading process. It is therefore important that a trader lets go of this emotion because failure to it will make a trader exit the market.

## Greed

For a trader to be considered a good trader, it is not only because he is strategic. Being a successful trader means that your account can back you up, therefore most people are so eager to have so much money in their account. Greed will most times result in a trader wanting to overtrade. The trade will tend to go against all the odds to overtrade in order to get more money. This will make even the trader will also take unreasonable risks that cannot be controlled in the long run. While taking risks is good for a trader, it is highly damaging when you are taking risks that are beyond you as a trader. Greed will often lead to overconfidence which will, in the long run, lead to a downfall. Overconfidence makes a person ignore all the trading basics, and therefore in the long term, the trader will be forced out.

Most traders make the mistake of being in the trading market without a proper plan. Trading is a business; without a plan, there is no success. Traders also the mistake of not knowing how to handle their money correctly, a trader may make a lot of money, but without proper management, you will lose it all. Sometimes traders will rely significantly on tip-offs before making the decision. This will not work out all the time, and it is damaging because as a trader, you don't give yourself enough opportunities to grow.

All traders need to have a proper goal as that is what will keep them on their toes and encourage them to stick in the market for long. A well-defined goal wills you the calmness and the right state of mind to keep fighting even when things get tough.

# Chapter 23: Why Those with the Right Mindset Become Successful Traders

Making it in the trading market does not require you to be highly educated with a college degree. A successful trader also does not need to spend all their day working to achieve it in the market. What makes a trader successful in their state of mind? In trade, you need to combine a great strategy with an excellent state of mind as this will help a trader gain confidence in all their transactions. Mindset is how your emotions and thoughts make you respond to issues. We generally react to problems due to how our mind is set up, and that's why it is essential to have the right mindset to be able to make great decisions. That is why to achieve anything, all we truly need is the right mindset that will encourage us to push on despite the many challenges we are likely to encounter along the way. The right state of mind gives calmness that later results in a trader being able to make decisions that are free of any emotions. Without emotions, a trader is able to look at the market at all angles without being forced to fall on one side. You appreciate the wins and all the profits you get as a trader you are aware you earned it by putting your hard work into it. You also take the losses positively to be a lesson for you so that you know what to do and what not to do in the future. Therefore as a trader, you can take responsibility for all the decisions you make.

Successful traders understand why it is essential to keep away their emotions from trading. Trading can be taught, and anyone can make it in the market, but who stays in the market is determined by their ability to separate the two. Being an emotionless trader means that not only do you make stable decisions, but you are also very accountable as a trader. You will never place blame on anyone or anything for your mistakes because you know you did your best it's only the circumstances that weren't favorable.

When the trader has the right mindset, it also means that they make the right realistic goals. A trader does not become too over-ambitious, making rational decisions that will not yield any results. Having set realistic goals means that your strategies as a trader are practical; therefore, there will be no time wasting trying to figure out the market. You already know what to expect from the market, and the market is also ready for you to make you a successful trader. Your expectations as a trader are also very realistic. You only take risks that you are aware of as a trader you can handle. A person who is not in their right state of mind will take risks that are way beyond him and then lose his mind when things don't work out.

Having the right state of mind makes a trader successful because they then get to understand how unique they are. This means there will be no comparison with other traders because this is often a way to failing. When you always compare your success with other traders, you are likely to be discouraged because each one has different levels of success. A successful trader will believe so much in themselves that there will be no room for this type of comparison. When you believe in yourself, it means that you believe in every single decision you make and therefore you will approach every trade with so much confidence.

A successful trader has patience which is only achieved when you have the right state of mind that gives calmness. Traders become successful when they can wait for the markets to show them when it is time to make various positions. A trader will have the patience to wait for profits to generate without feeling like they are pressured to take whatever comes along. A successful trader also has the patience to accept the losses; their right state of mind tells them to grab the loss as a learning lesson. Therefore the trader will use the endurance to overcome all the hard market situations.

The right state of mind enables a trader to overcome the emotion of greed. He can identify when he is a good trader who wants to make the right money and when he is just a greedy trader. A greedy trader makes closes on trades when it is too soon because they want to make profits regardless of how small the amount is. They, therefore, make many closes instead of being patient for the earnings to grow before making the close. A successful trader accepts that there is power in letting go of a loss. However, a greedy trader will overwork trying to make up for past failures and forgetting to focus on the present.

The right state of mind helps a trader become successful because it eliminates the fear of taking risks. While other traders are trying to be careful thinking they taking risks will put them at a losing end, a trader with the right state of mind will go for it. The right state of mind helps a trader knows that to make it in the market, there have to be huge risks that one has to face. There is no fear of failure for a person with the right state of mind because the trader knows that part of the trading process.

The right state of mind makes a person a successful trader because it gives a person the ability to let go of the past. Most people fail as traders because they are stuck in the past, always trying to mend the past when what they should be doing is dealing with the present. A right state of mind enables a trader to focus on what they can do to improve their present and also on how to prepare for the future.

Successful traders are traders whose right state of mind encouraged them to keep learning no matter how excellent they felt. This is what distinguishes successful long-term traders and successful short-term traders. While short-term traders achieved for a while and relaxed, the long term trader continued learning and therefore got to their current successful state.

# Chapter 24: Mistakes to Avoid on the Expiration Day

Options trading only gives you the freedom to sell or buy securities before the expiration of the options. Options usually lose their value as they approach their expiration day. This kind of trade is sometimes very volatile and its expiration date may be very hard to be predetermined. This, therefore, makes options traders commit some mistakes on the expiration day of the trade that makes them make losses. There are various mistakes that a vigilant trader should at all cost try to avoid on their trade's expiration day. These mistakes are discussed below;

- **Forgetting when the trade is set to expire**

    Different options trades have different rules that determine their expiration day. On opening a trade, one's main aim is usually to make a profit. Some individuals once they make profits, tend to forget to exit the trade yet it has approached its expiration day. On the other hand, if one had made losses, they may tend to leave the trade open as they try to get some of their money back which might never happen. As the trade approaches its expiration date, it is a fact that it loses its value faster. Therefore, the chances of one making more profit from the trade are very few. To avoid losing your trading capital, it is safer to close your options trade and claim your losses or profits before the trade close.

- **Exercising your options**

    In case you own options and the expiration day is approaching, then you should never dare to exercise them. It is advisable not to own stocks whenever you purchase options unless if you are taking on an options strategy or a stock. If you have a strong urge to own stock as you buy options, then you should plan earlier. Failure to do so then you will be making losses and it will have no difference with throwing it away into thrash. Several options traders, especially beginners, purchasing options are not the best approach to owning shares.

    In case the prices of stock increases by a good margin that is enough to recover the premiums paid, then you will have made a profit. This does not matter when it comes to a person who purchases options intending to own shares at a later time. There are many exceptions but it is advisable not to exercise your options on the expiration day. Instead, you should sell the options if you do not feel like owning again. Exercising options on their expiration day will not make you any profit but instead, you might lose it all.

- **Margin calls on the expiration day**

  Beginners in options trading, especially those owning small accounts, usually fall into the purchase of options. The purchase of options is not an issue but they fail to understand the trading rules thus fail to sell out their options before the expiration day. If an options trader owns five August 40 calls and does not make an effort to sell them, it would be fine for the person to let them expire worthless. On the other hand, if a trader does not closely watch out and allows the trade to close at $40.02 on its expiration, then the trader will now own 500 shares. If the trade closes with more money by a penny or more on its expiration day, then the options are usually exercised automatically.

  On the next Monday after expiration day, the 500 shares the trader now owns will come with a margin call. Since the trader did not know that he or she was going to purchase stock, they will lack enough money in their accounts to pay the shares. They will, therefore, be forced to sell the shares. It is thus very important to avoid this mistake of failing to sell long options before the expiration day.

- **Fear of Assignment notice**

  As an options trader, you should never fear when assigned to an exercise notice for an option that you sold. If you are prepared then you should never fear provided it does not result in a margin call. On selling an option, you should be able to understand that the owner of the option can exercise it any time before its expiration day at will. This should, therefore, be neither surprised nor a problem when it happens. Writing a covered call, you are assigned guarantees to the trade's maximum profit.

In case you make a sale of options that has got no position in the stock, then you should be sure to meet margin calls if you are assigned an exercise notice. It will be the work of your broker to supply an answer if you are not able to personally figure it out. This case should not, however, freak you out. It is very beneficial to get an assignment notice before expiration day as it reduces the risks associated with the trade. Fear of assignment notice is, therefore, one of the mistakes that should be avoided before the expiration day.

- **Failure to differentiate how European-Style Options expire**

  Unlike any other type of option, European-style options usually expire on the third Thursday of every month as compared to other options that expire on each third Friday. This is the most common mistake that is committed especially by new options traders. If you have a plan of closing your trade on its expiration day then fail to consider the time difference, then your options might expire without your knowledge. This might result in big losses to options traders. You might never know that your options expired until the time when the settlement price shall be determined. The settlement price is usually determined either in the early Thursday afternoon or Friday morning. You should, therefore, avoid this kind of mistake by closing your trades on Thursdays before their expiration. It is very vital to create a reminder if you doubt that you can remember to do so in time. The reminder would alert you and thus be able to close the European options trade on time before it expires.

# Chapter 25: Other Strategies for Beginners in Option Trading

Before venturing into options trading, it is vital to have a plan of action. Options trading has of late become very popular since it gives individuals a chance to make money fast. This does not mean that no losses occur but one can also lose large amounts of money fast. Options trading strategies range from simple to complex ones with a variety of odd names and payoffs. The simple strategies already discussed include long call, covered call, long put, short put and married put. These strategies had been earlier discussed thus we will discuss other different strategies for beginners in options trading. These strategies are more complex as compared to the previous ones and are discussed below;

# Long Straddle Strategy

This options strategy is where an options trader purchases both long put and long call for the same asset having a similar strike price and expiration date. This strategy entails benefitting from unpredictable and big moves. This strategy is said to be complex due to the sophisticated calculations that are done by options traders. This strategy aims at making profits from any outcome but also has challenges just like any other investment. Risks associated with this strategy is that the market might not react to the event generated by it strongly enough. This, therefore, makes this strategy expensive since it entails investing in two approaches.

This strategy can alternatively be used in capturing the expected increase in the trade's volatility. Implied volatility is very influential when determining the prices of options. An increase in the volatility, therefore, means that there is an increase in all options' prices. This strategy is characterized by limited risks and unlimited profits. In case the prices of the stock increase continually, then the advantages expected are limited. On the other hand, if the prices of the stock become zero, then the profit is the difference between the strike price and the premiums that were paid for the purchased options.

## Buy-Write Strategy

This strategy is also referred to as the covered call strategy. This strategy is majorly employed on stocks. An example of this strategy is the sales of covered calls. This strategy entails the purchase of stocks then the investor sells the stock's call options. The main purpose of this strategy is the generation of income from the premiums paid for options. This strategy works by making assumptions that the security's market price would change and might rise before its expiration day. On the other hand, if the option's price declines, the investor would then write a call to keep premiums from the sale of options. This strategy may be used to increase returns by periodically repeating it when the time for the options is lackluster.

To implement this strategy accurately, the option's strike price should always be higher as compared to the price of the stock. This, therefore, needs well-executed judgment as the strike price should be higher but not as to make the premium price insignificant. If the expiration period is set to be prolonged then this means that the premiums will also be high. This strategy might lose its position in case the price of options rises rapidly.

## Married Put Strategy

This strategy is also referred to as a synthetic long call. Married put strategy is an options trading strategy that entails the trader purchasing put options together with shares equivalent to the purchased stock. This strategy is commonly employed in cases where the investor acts bullish on certain stocks and might want to benefit from the stock. Its profit potential is unlimited and is similar to that of the long call. This strategy also has got a limited risk which is usually calculated by the addition of the premium paid to the commissions paid. The break-even point of this strategy is achieved by determining the underlying price. The break-even point is determined by adding the premium paid to the price of underlying securities. This strategy works similarly as an insurance cover having certain strike-price and is against the short-term losses. At the same time frame, the options trader would the very call options at an increased strike price.

## Protective Collar Strategy

This strategy is where an options trader purchase shares of a given option then sell a short call option and simultaneously purchases a long put to limit downside risks. This strategy majorly aims at the protection of stocks that have got a low market price. Protective collar strategy employs call options upon its sale and puts options upon purchase. In this case, both put options and call options should have a similar number of shares and expiration date.

This strategy entails the integration of short call, long put options, and long stocks. In options trading, a long stock refers to where a trader purchased underlying assets hoping to earn from them in the future. When employing this strategy, it is advisable to take a long put option if the market price might continuously fall and you want to prevent further loss of money and limit risks.

An advantage of this strategy is that it is cheap as compared to the purchase of protective put in instances where you will have to sell out your money from your shares. On the other hand, this strategy might be disadvantageous since the profits are limited in instances where the price of stock increases. The protective collar strategy works well with the protection of profits obtained from stock.

## Long Strangle Strategy

This strategy is neutral and it entails simultaneously purchasing an out-of-the-money call and out-of-the-money put having a similar expiration date and the underlying stock. This strategy is characterized by limited risks and unlimited profits gained from the stocks. This is obtained where the options trader believes that the stock would experience significant volatility. This strategy is a debit spread since debit is usually taken so that one can enter this trade. The large profits for this strategy are usually obtained in cases where the price of an underlying stock fluctuates at expiration day. The maximum loss for this strategy is obtained by adding the total premiums paid to the commissions paid.

# Chapter 26: The Best Strategies to Invest with Call and Put Options Trading

An option is a contract that provides an opportunity to an investor either to purchase or sell an underlying commodity as security at a particular price over a given time period. There is a market where the purchasing and selling of these options, which is options trading, is carried out. This market is referred to as the options market. Options trading basically involves trading in options and are particularly involved with securities of stock or even bond market. These options are classified into two, namely, call option and put option. A call option is when a buyer of a contract holds the right to buy purchase an underlying asset at a price predetermined for the future. On the other hand, a put option is when a buyer purchases the right to allow him or her sell an underlying asset at a price predetermined for a future time. It is also important to note that the trade options are better preferred compared to the direct assets. This is because there exist some advantages to trading options. These advantages include providing increased cost efficiency, they are of less risk to direct assets such as stocks and most importantly they provide some strategic alternatives. The right to buy or sell options is viable to an investor throughout until the date of expiration. There are very many strategies that an investor can use when participating in options trading. These strategies vary depending on the reward, risk among other factors. Below are some strategies to invest with call and put options trading;

- **Go for a covered call**

    This strategy involves purchasing a call option that is referred to as naked. This strategy lowers some of the risks that could result in the investor becoming alone long stock. It also generates income for the investor. The compromise to this particular strategy is that an investor must be willing to sell the shares at a price that is a short strike. In order to carry out the strategy, you have to buy an underlying stock as you would normally, and at the same time sell the same shares on the call option.

- **Married put**

    Here the investor buys an asset, for example, stock shares, while at the same time purchasing an equal number of put options involving shares. This strategy safeguards an investor's downside risk at the time they are holding stock shares, thus any investor prefers to use it. If it happens that the price of a stock begins falling sharply, this strategy creates a base price. Basically, for this strategy it is appealing to an investor since it offers protection from the downside should there be any negative occurring event. Likewise, if there be any upside from stocks gaining value at any time, the investor benefits fully from it. This strategy, however, has one disadvantage, whereby the investor will lose the amount paid as premium for put option if the value of the stock does not reduce.

- **Bull Call Spread**

    A bull call spread is our third strategy to invest with call and put options trading. Under this strategy, an investor simultaneously purchases calls at a certain price and sell the equivalent quantity of calls at a strike price that is higher than the amount he or she used for buying them. The underlying asset is the same for the two call options as is the expiration. This type of strategy is referred to as being vertically spread. It is used when there is a bullish investor who also is expecting that any rise in the asset price should be moderate.

- **Bear put spread**

    This strategy of a bear put spread is actually the opposite of the bull call spread in terms of explanation but involves the put options. An investor will buy put options at a certain strike price and simultaneously sell that same amount of puts at a price that is lower than the buying strike price. Similarly, to the bull call spread, both of the options will be having the same underlying assets and expiration dates. This is a strategy used by a trader or an investor who expects a decline in price for the underlying asset and at the same time is bearish. It provides gains and losses that are both limited.

- **Long Call Butterfly spread**

    In this strategy, it combines two other strategies, which are the bear spread and bull spread strategies. However, it uses three strike prices that are completely different from each other. The underlying asset and date of expiration are the same for all options. An investor ends up using this strategy when he or she thinks that the expiration for the stock will most definitely not experience a big move change. Maximum loss under this strategy happens when the stock is either below or at a lower strike, or if it settles above or at the strike call that is highest. Both the upside and downside of this strategy are limited.

- **Long call strategy**

  Here a person purchases a call option. This strategy stakes at the price of an underlying stock rising by expiration above the set strike price. This strategy is used by an investor who is not bothered about losing an entire premium by staking on the rising of stock such that he or she could receive greater profit than if they directly owned the stock.

- **Long put strategy**

  This strategy is very similar to the sixth above only that for this case one wagers on the decline of stock rather than a rise. An investor purchases a put option, counting on the stock to fall by expiration below the strike price. Under this strategy the investor sacrifices to lose the full premium, waging that the stock will decline. If it happens that stock decline, an investor ends earning much by owning puts than he or she would have by selling the stock.

# Chapter 27: Describe Examples of Trade

There are many types of trades in a financial market that one can choose from. These trades require an intensified prior research and in-depth understanding before setting your foot into any of them. However, one is advised to try to master one specific trade that they are comfortable with. It is, however, advisable to be proficient in other trades as well. This is to enable you to find that specific trade that best suits your specific interests and one that you find having a higher probability to provide you more profits. This provides you with the opportunity to analyze them and make the right decisions on which type of trade you will invest in. These different types of trade focus on the sale of securities, stocks, etc. In this chapter, the five main types of trade are explained in depth.

# Position Trading

It simply means taking a position in an asset with the anticipation of joining a larger market trend or rather expecting that the asset may increase in value over a given period of time. Position trading does not put much emphasis on the minor price fluctuation or market corrections that have the tendency of reversing the price trend temporarily. The long term performance of the various assets in the market is the positional trader's main concern. Their main aim while in the market is to analyze that specific trend in the price of securities that can relatively go for a long period. Position trading can provide very high returns amidst the high transaction costs involved. It also has the advantage that it does not require a lot of the trader's time, once the trade has been made and necessary market strategies put in place, then once you only require to wait for the outcome. However, it is also associated with substantive risk especially in cases where there is an unforeseen trend reversal or rather in cases of low liquidity. Generally, positional trading revolves around the utilization of fundamental and technical analysis. An options trader is usually at liberty to use both methods to ensure that he/she makes sound decisions.

# Day Trading

This involves the sale and purchase of securities in just a single day. This trade can go for hours or even minutes. Day trading is most of the time characterized by an easy way of getting rich, however, day traders suffer great losses within a day. They usually make short term strategies to benefit from small fluctuations in prices. Day traders usually exit the market before the market closes to avoid getting risks. This method of trading can be applied in any type of trade through it is quite common in the foreign exchange market. It is a requirement that you be well updated on the current news so as to benefit from day trading. This is because these emerging issues are the reason for the small price movements. They include various announcements such as corporate earnings, interest rates or economic statistics among others. The technique used in this trade is the intraday strategy. These strategies include scalping which tends to make small profits based on small price fluctuations throughout the day. Range trading which usually uses resistance levels to determine they buy or sell decisions, New based trading basically captures trading opportunities from market volatilities resulting from news events. The high-frequency trading strategies which basically use algorithms to identify short term market inefficiencies.

## Scalping

This involves obtaining very small profits repeatedly. This type of trading usually takes advantage of accruing small profits based on very small price fluctuations. Scalping trade is usually based on the anticipation that the majority of the stocks will complete the first stage of the movement. Its movement after the first step is however uncertain. The traders who carry out this type of trade are characterized by making numerous types of trades within a day. They work from the basis that these small shifts in prices are the easiest to capture as compared to the larger price fluctuations. This trade requires strict exits strategies however since the loses that one could incur might be huge enough to eliminate all the small gains that you may have accrued over some time. It may be so easy to lure people into this type of trade due to the thinking that it has returned, for beginners, it is not recommended as one may risk making very huge losses. This trade requires some kind of expertise and skills to succeed in it.

## Momentum Trading

In this trade, the traded focuses on making their buy or sell based on the strength of the recent price trends. The trader ensures that he/she makes the trade at the point where there is maximum momentum on either the upstream or the downstream. Most of the times they put more focus on that stock which follows one direction on a high volume. This type of trade usually lasts from several hours to a few days based on how swiftly the stock moves and at what instance it changes direction. The strategies employed in this trade are usually both short and long term. While investing in momentum trading, one holds the belief that a particular trend persists until its conclusion and that it is possible to profit from as long as you stay with the trend.

## Swing Trading

This type of trade involves holding a tradable asset for a period of one to several weeks with the aim of making profits from the price changes. Swing traders can use both technical and fundamental analysis to capture trade opportunities as well as in analyzing the trends of market prices and patterns. Usually, the main goal is to capture a high potential price move and then move on to the next opportunity. This type of trade has the tendency to expose the trader with the risk of making huge losses in cases where a closed session opens up with a substantially different price. Usually, the swing traders use a set of mathematically based rules for making trades to eliminate various technicalities when making the buy or sell decisions. Other strategies used include the Alexander Elder's strategy. This strategy measures the behavior of an asset price trend using three different moving averages.

# Chapter 28. Probable Tips and Suggestions to Try to Succeed with Options Trading

Becoming an options trader who consistently enjoys success in his endeavors is not just something that you find yourself achieving overnight. You require to spice the process by bringing in new ideas and concepts that may seem probable. When these tips are incorporated in the right way you will surely find yourself up the ladder of success with a lot of ease. This article will equip you with some of these tips that you may use to your advantage.

One of the key tips is in ensuring that you focus on the prices of the options. You realize that options grow more and more worthless as time goes by simply because at the end of it all they will finally expire. This is a characteristic shared by all the options, no exception. The majority of the option traders make the mistake of laying so much emphasis on studying the market as well as the stock. They usually make their decisions on whether to buy or sell their options based on this. They often forget the prices of these options. You should always focus on buying low-priced options and sell the high-priced options. Being able to differentiate the low-priced options from the cheap options in the market is one of the steps towards success in options trading. A low-priced option usually provides a very high return. Failure to consider this factor of options prices may just make you end up accumulating losses. When the options are well thought of and analyzed properly they can be very rewarding.

Another tip is to ensure that you have the necessary tools to stay in the market. Your risk management strategies should be well outlined. Your option trade can turn out to be the most successful if you manage your risks appropriately. However, the majority of the option traders usually focus on the amount of money they plan on getting and forget the loses they risk accumulating. You realize that most of the decisions that you make in option trading will be influenced by this factor. As for the case of the amount of capital that you would invest, you would only risk investing that amount that you would bear to lose in case things worked against you. Most of the option trading strategies, however, are quite risky. But you can try out various risk management strategies so as to minimize loses as much as possible. Enormous loses have the potential of affecting you for even a whole month or even make you exit the trade.

Creating a good game plan that is quite quantifiable is a major tip in ensuring success in options trading. Make sure that the goals outlined in the strategy are quite clear and realistic. They should not set the bar too high or rather appear in achievable in any way. With a clear strategy, you are able to focus on the latter. Your strategy should also be strict in a way that asses all the aspects of your options trading. Ensure that you also exercise the virtue of discipline to your course so as you reap success in an options trade. Your game plan should also be quite flexible to accommodate the changing market patterns.

It is quite advisable to trade with a well-known stock or rather one that you are quite familiar with. By this, you are able to even predict the price movements of stock. This is usually a very crucial exercise that can reap you maximum benefits. You also do not have to go through a lot of struggles on analyzing the stock as you are already familiar with them. However, there is a need to ensure that you consistently do a lot of market research on the same to keep up with the changing trends. For well-known stock, the majority of them enjoy huge volumes and have the tendency to remain in the market for longer periods.

The other tip is on the choice of an options trade broker. It is wise to ensure that they offer you with quite affordable or rather user-friendly commissions. High commissions will affect your profitability as well as your strategy. Nonetheless, do not go for the low fee brokers if they are not in a position to offer you reliable services like better trading opportunities as well as saving you time. Failure to which you may end up losing much of your dollars due to their inefficiency. For online brokers, ensure that they have convenient methods or platforms that can enable easy transfer of money. This decision on the choice of a broker is a decision worth spending a lot of time on. The success of your trade highly depends on the broker you chose.

It is quite possible to think that your psychology does not play a key role in the options trade. Many options traders overlook this and end up making decisions that ruin their trades completely. This is quite common especially when you make huge losses and become emotional. This is very normal and expected but you should learn that any decision you make while in this state of mind may completely work against you. It is therefore advisable to learn how to react to such losses. Moreover, try as much as possible to combat the fear of losing. This may refrain you from enjoying huge profits that you could have earned in case you entered the trade.

Ensure that you take advantage of market volatility. Many new traders have the tendency to overlook this critical factor. They do forget that it is not always that options will reflect the move that a particular stock will take. It is advisable to understand how market volatility affects the implied price of the option. In the case where there are susceptible high market volatility and consecutive huge moves. It is quite advisable to use the straddle strategy. This refers to the buying of the call and the put option at a particular strike price for a given period of time. It usually has the advantage of providing limited risks.

# Chapter 29: Possible Errors to Avoid That Can Be Committed in Option Trading

When trading options, it is possible to lose money that you have invested and it is therefore important to be aware of errors that can be made when trading. They include lack of a strategy in exiting the market, trading in options that are not liquid among other mistakes that will be comprehensively discussed below.

# Buying into the Option of the Out-Of-The-Money Call Options

In the options market, buying into the out-of-money options is one of the most difficult means of making money. Such call options are always inviting to new traders for in most cases they are always less expensive than other options. What most new traders do that make them lose money is enacting this strategy only, which does not give successful, consistent gains.

## Lack of a Strategy in Trading

When a trader does not have a strategy in entering and exiting the market, there is a high possibility to make losses. Without a strategy, a trader will not know when to make a trade, and with what amount of money. A chance may, therefore, pass you when you've got no plan for your trading. Before buying or selling an option, make a clear cut and concise plan, to avoid making mistakes when trading, that would have otherwise been avoided.

## Lack of a Strategy in Exiting the Market

Some traders lack an exit plan suitable for when they are making losses and conversely when they are making profits. An exit plan is to provide a solution when you want to close a trade. Without one, you will not know the appropriate time to close down a trade, which may leave you open to making huge losses in the market, when you don't close the trade early enough and reversed profits to losses when the markets reverse.

## Not Putting into Consideration, the Expiry Date

Not have a prediction made on the time frame that a trade will go may prove to be loss-making. In trading options, making a prediction on how long trade of an option will take is a key aspect. Factors such as reports on earnings are crucial in determining the expiry date. Traders may fail to make decisions on the correct expiry dates that correlate with the factor events, that makes their strategy to be useless at this point.

## Having so Much Leverage on the Trades Made

Traders who are mostly used to trading in the stocks market make the mistake of buying options with way too much money that is needed for options. Options are classified as derivatives and they do not, therefore, cost as much as the options. Large sums of leverage are therefore not needed in this category in the market, a mistake that many traders from the stock market are susceptible to doing. This opens up their trade to many losses, stemming from the unnecessarily high amount of leverage on the trades, such that when a trade does not go as intended, their whole strategy crumbles.

## Trading with the Less Expensive Options

Cheap options in the market, which some traders may prefer, turn out to be no money-making options. The mistake in trading in the cheap options is that they have low premiums, whose strike price will always be way above the cost going in the market or as well below the market costs. To counter such a difference in the prices, the trader is therefore forced to create a more drastic strategy to salvage the options traded. It is not a wise decision to always buy cheap options.

## Indecision on Early Options

The indecision that plagues some traders on the early options is always uncalled for. On an early option, some traders do not buy and sell the options in the right manner, according to the rights that they are accorded by the buyers. The indecision is always rooted in a panic on what to do with the options. They do not know at what appropriate time to close their losing trades and let the gaining ones remain open, without panicking over the possibility of the market reversing and them making losses thereafter.

## Trading with the Wrong Size of a Trade

The portfolios that some traders have do not always go hand in hand with the size of the trades that they make. In one case scenario, they can be risking too much in trading risky options, whereby if they make losses, their portfolios cannot cover them. On the other hand, they can be making a trade that is way too risky, where they lose on trades that would've made gains, and the portfolios are well capable of covering that, the most common case under this mistake is the traders risking all of their portfolios. They do not think about the question of whether they can afford to risk the amount of money traded if the trades made losses.

## Maximizing on a Losing Trade

Maintaining a losing trade for a long period of time is one of the mistakes that traders are highly susceptible to making. Riding on a losing trade that will just result in losses is of no good. When the indicator shows high levels of losses, traders do not exit the trade, with prospects that the trade will reverse. They do not distinguish between losing trades that do not reverse and the ones that can have the possibility of reversing from proper analysis.

# Trading in Options That Are Not Liquid

This is a mistake that costs traders when they want to close a losing trade and at the same time much money than if the option would have been liquid. An illiquid option does not give the leeway to buy and sell options in a quick manner, therefore exiting the market when the trader's desires become difficult. Most of the traders who trade in options that are not liquid do not often check on the opening interest on the option. Most of the options that are illiquid will have less interest, thus less flexible that these with larger interests, usually the larger companies.

# Chapter 30: The Conclusion on What Was Written and the Goodness of the Book

You are at the end of the book: *Options Trading for Beginners Book Outline* and thank you for reading through it and making it to the end. Let's be hopeful that it has been helpful enough to provide the knowledge and skills that are needed to start trading in options as a newbie in the market. And as not everything might have been covered in this book outline, it would also be great if you would seek to enrich yourself with such knowledge from other sources apart from this book. The book has nonetheless covered great subjects on the introduction of the options market to a new and a beginner trader that seeks to apprentice the reader to the market. Written in this outline, as you've read, is a comprehensive guide to starting trading in options.

As the main subject of the book is, the basics of options trading have been greatly discussed, offering the reader a clear picture of what options reading in general is. The points outlined at the opening chapter break down the options market in chunks that a beginner can well relate to. It also piques up your interest to find more about options trading and how they operate in making money. You are also encouraged to start on trading options by the book outlining the advantages of the trade that leaves you motivated to start on it already. You are made aware of the fundamentals of the trade and the components of it, further expanding your knowledge of the options market, which will prove to be very helpful to a beginner in the market, for they are well aware of what options trading comprises of.

The highlight of the book to the reader is talking about how to get started in trading the options. This part offers you the practical skills and gears you up to take the first step in making your beginner trade. The knowledge written in this book would be to naught if you, the reader, who is a beginner trader, would not make the first trade, following care guidelines. And this book has just done that. Written down great and helpful tactics to kick you off as you start your journey in the options trading world. After gaining such skills, employ them in the real market world and get to experience the highs and the lows, but as stated in the book, nonetheless great strategies.

As a beginner in trading, you have also benefited from other aspects written in the book such as risk and risk management; very crucial, leverage, and others such as technical analysis. These aspects will be vital in trading, for in most cases that determine the profitability of the trades that you have made. Let's hope that you have gone through these aspects carefully and taken away the key points that will be crucial when you are trading. Factors such as leverage will distinguish you from becoming a professional trader in no time and a trader who makes mistakes and errors that would have otherwise been avoided. Technical analysis in the book has been discussed extensively as one of the key issues to dwell on when you begin trading. As observed in the book, it can be termed as the backbone that holds the trading. It is the most important takeaway you can take. Without the analysis, your takeoff as a beginner trader would be baseless, for you would be making assumptions on the market without any reference, which is a suicidal thing to do in the market.

Of great import to traders in this book outline as they progress from being beginners is the subject of psychology in trading. The book has delved deeper into the emotional outplay in options trading, where the thoughts in this chapter seek to elevate you to a higher state of emotional approach towards trading in options. We are hopeful that you will be able to learn from this outline the importance of trading with your emotions kept in check, as the book advertises, for successful trading. Apply this knowledge in real-time trading and approach the market in the right mental state, this being one of the skills that were mentioned in the psychology of options trading. It will do you good to be well conversant in this section as a beginner.

As a beginner, probably the most exciting part of the book was where tips on succeeding in options trading were extensively written down. This should buoy your beginner trading spirits up and gear you up for being successful in this field, which you'll be, after following the tips outlined here and from many other sources. To be fully confident in your trading capacities and abilities, this outline had also provided in text form of the mistakes that are to be avoided when you are trading.

All this said, it remains up to you, the beginner reader of trading in options to make the most crucial move; and that is making your first trade. This should not be procrastinated as the book has prepared you enough for the market, and you should be confident to make trades, and also make it a learning experience from your gains and losses, which are a sure thing to make in trading. Also, be sure to get useful information from enlightening sources to keep you on top-notch. We hope the skills that you've gathered from this awesome book will prove to be helpful as you start trading and making your way in options trading. We wish you the best of luck as you start on this enthralling endeavor in your life, packed with all the information you need. May you make the best trades and predictions with this outline as your guiding ray.

Thank you for taking your time to go through this outline and if you found the contents of this book to be helpful in any way, please do a review of it in any platform, which will be highly appreciated.

# Description

What could be the basics options of trading? What are the types of options trading? What are the advantages of trading in option? What are the components of an option contract? What are the fundamentals of the pricing options? How do you start trading in options? What are some of the tools required for trading? What are some of the risks of leverage? What are the advantages and disadvantages of trading leverage options? How much does it take to trade-in option? How can one trade intelligently? What are some of the features of technical analysis? What are the different types of graphs that could exist? What are some of the strategies that could be applied with technical analysis? How do one control emotions? What are some of the basics of psychology in trading options? What are some of the examples of trade? What could be the possible tips and suggestions that could be borrowed for success? What are some of the possible errors that can be avoided in options trading?

Options trading is meant to direct one on when there is more profit in the market and when the market is not making any progress at all. It will act as a tool that will provide leverage and will give possible accounts of how the market of the commodities is fairing on the outside. The option trading is supposed to be the contract between two parties who have sat and have to discuss what is entailed in the contract document and are now reading on the same script or have agreed on the terms of the contract. We have two types of options trading they are puts and calls.

Some of the reasons why we have trading options are that it acts as a form of insurance. You cannot put all your eggs in one basket. That is why it is recommended that you get the insurance that will protect what you have invested in. the other reason is that it will bring income to you. This happens when there is some sort of selling to other individuals you will be making some income. The other reason is that you will have limited some of the risks that you may encounter because you will have put in place several strategies to curb any type of risk.

The goal of this book is to ensure you understand the various options of trading. This book will give guidelines on how to go about the options trading.

**In this book, you will learn:**

- The Basics of Options Trading
- Types of Trading Option
- Advantages of Trading in Option
- Components of Trading in Option Contract
- Fundamentals of the Pricing Option
- Starting Trading in Options
- Platforms and Tools for Trading Options Leverage
- Why Leverage Can be Riskier

- The Advantages and Disadvantages of Trading Leverage Option
- How Much Leverage it Takes to Trade in Options
- How You Can Manage Risk in Options Trading.
- How You Can Trade Options Intelligently.
- The Support and Resistances
- The Different Features of Technical Analysis
- The Different Types of Graphs Used for Technical Analysis
- Strategies and Risk That Can be Applied in the Technical Analysis
- How to Control Emotions and Have the Right Mindset
- Describe Examples of Trade
- The Probable Tips and Suggestions to Succeed with the Option
- Possible Errors to Avoid that Can be Committed in Option Trading

Would you like to Know More?

Download this book and get equipped with all the information you need about options trading.

**Scroll to the top of the page and select the buy now button.**

Made in the USA
Middletown, DE
23 June 2020